OUT OF
THE ARK

OUT OF THE ARK

Stories from the World's Religions

Anita Ganeri
Illustrated by Jackie Morris

MACDONALD YOUNG BOOKS

This edition first published in Great Britain in 1994
by Simon & Schuster Young Books

Reprinted in 1997 by Macdonald Young Books, an imprint of
Wayland Publishers Limited
61 Western Road
Hove
East Sussex
BN3 1JD

First printed in paperback by Macdonald Young Books in 1998

Find Macdonald Young Books on the internet at
http://www.myb.co.uk

To Tim Stowe (J.M)
To my brothers (A.G)

Designed by Martin Lovelock
Printed in Portugal

British Library Cataloguing in Publication Data available

ISBN 0 7500 2667 7

Contents

INTRODUCTION

T his is a collection of stories from some of the world's greatest religions and faiths. Most of these are 'living' religions, still practised by millions of people all over the world. (Just occasionally, a story from an ancient religion long since dead has also slipped in!) All these religions are treasure chests of stories. Some stories relate episodes from the lives of the gods, great leaders or historical figures. Other stories have a message or a moral. Still others explain events that could not be understood scientifically at the time, such as the creation of the world, or the great flood. Religious teachers have always used stories as a way to hold people's attention, and to get their message across.

This book has been divided up into sections, each with its own theme such as Creation, or Courtship or the Great Flood. You will see that similar themes often crop up in more than one religion. For example, the story of the great flood sent by the gods to punish the human race for its wickedness is found in the Christian and Jewish faiths, in Islam and Hinduism, and in ancient beliefs such as those from Babylon. As these religions spread their influence further afield, so they spread their stories. To begin with, these stories were not written down but passed on by word of mouth. They probably found their way to other countries and cultures by means of travelling storytellers and traders.

Wherever a story comes from, and whatever message it carries with it, its magic lies in provoking your thoughts and capturing your imagination. I hope that this selection of stories will do just that, and that you will have pleasure reading them.

BAIAME, THE GREAT SPIRIT

Thousands and thousands of years ago in Australia there was a time known as Dreamtime. This was when the spirits lived on Earth with the people and animals, and the landscape took its shape. The emu-men, bowerbird-women, kangaroo-men and fig-men roamed far and wide, and their actions formed the hills and the waterholes, the trees and the caves.

The Earth itself, say the Aborigines, was created by the great spirit, Baiame. He made the land and the sky, the sun, the moon and the stars. At first, the Earth was flat and the sky came down so close to the land that there was no room in-between for birds to fly, or for people and animals to grow. Everything that lived on the Earth was the size of an ant – even Baiame. Another strange thing was that there were no lakes or rivers. There was just one, single waterhole and even Baiame had forgotten exactly where it was, it was so well hidden.

One day, quite by chance, Baiame found the waterhole. He bathed in its cool water and took a long, welcome drink. Now, the waterhole was filled with magic water and, as Baiame drank, he became filled with magic too. Then he set about putting the world to rights. He lifted his arms and, with all his strength, pushed the sky upwards until it formed an arch above the land – just as it does today. There was plenty of room now for the birds to fly, and for people and animals to grow tall. Baiame himself grew bigger and bigger, leaving it to the ants to be ant-sized, as they alone should be.

Now that the sky was in its proper place, clouds could form in it and rain could fall from it to make rivers and lakes. The dry, brown earth bloomed with grass, flowers and trees. People were full of praise for the great thing Baiame had done. Then Baiame made himself a camp high up in the sky, called Bullima. From his camp, he could look down at all the things he had made and he was quite content with what he saw.

Down on Earth, however, all was not well. The flowers were not happy because they wanted to be with Baiame. So one night, under cover of darkness, they crept up to Bullima and made it the most beautiful, most colourful place in the world. Imagine the consternation when people woke up the next morning to find that all the flowers had gone. They searched for them high and low but the flowers were nowhere to be found. It was the saddest day there had ever been. And it wasn't just the people who missed the flowers. The bees couldn't find any flower pollen so they couldn't make any honey. The butterflies couldn't find any flower nectar so they had nothing to eat.

Then the old men of the tribes called a meeting to decide what to do.

'We have no choice,' they said. 'We must go to Bullima and ask the great spirit for his help.' Nobody had a better idea, so the next day the old men set off on the long journey to find Baiame. To reach his camp in the sky, they had to climb the highest mountain in all of Australia. It was steep and jagged and many a time they nearly gave up. They climbed for five days and nights until at last they saw Baiame's beautiful camp, decked in flowers. Baiame was surprised to see the old men but he invited them in and listened to their tale. There was just one problem. He wanted to help them but, at the same time, he couldn't bear the thought of the flowers leaving. So he considered the problem for a long time, and finally he hit upon an answer.

'Pick as many flowers as you can carry,' he told the old men, 'and take them back to Earth. Scatter them on the ground and leave them to take root. They will die in the hot, dry summer – but every spring they will grow again.'

The old men thanked Baiame and began to gather up bundles of flowers. Then they started the long journey home. To their astonishment, the flowers stayed as fresh as if they had just been picked. When they reached their camps they scattered the flowers on the ground, as Baiame had instructed them to do, and watched them take root and grow. Everyone was full of great joy. Children wove flower garlands; women threaded flowers into their hair. The bees buzzed about making honey and the butterflies lapped up the sweet, syrupy nectar.

When the summer came, Baiame's words came true. The flowers wilted and died. But, also true to his word, in spring the flowers bloomed again. Now everyone was happy – Baiame in his sky camp and the people and animals on Earth.

THE CHURNING OF THE SEA OF MILK

In the Hindu religion, the world is ruled by hundreds of gods and goddesses. The most important of these are the three gods of the trinity – Brahma the creator, Vishnu the preserver, and Shiva the destroyer. Lord Brahma, the four-headed, is the creator of the universe and father of both gods and men. Sometimes he sleeps and sometimes he wakes. While he sleeps, the universe is destroyed and does not exist. When he wakes, he creates the universe and everything in it anew. And so the cycle continues, in a never-ending progression of night and day, of destruction and creation.

The story goes that long ago, before the world began, there was nothing but a pure white lotus flower floating in a sea of milk. Inside its silky petals lay Lord Brahma, the creator, fast asleep. Outside the lotus flower, there was nothing to be seen. Then Lord Brahma stirred. He opened his eyes and, wide awake, began the task of creating the world. From his tears he made the land, the air and the sky. His outstretched body became the universe, day and night, darkness and light. He created the dry seasons and the monsoons, the fire, the wind and the rain. From his mouth came goats, from his sides, cows, and from his feet, elephants, camels, horses and deer. The hairs on his body became grasses, roots and fruits. And then Brahma created the Devas and Asuras – the gods of light and of darkness.

Now, the sea of milk contained a magical liquid, called amrita, the elixir of life. Anyone who drank amrita would live forever. Naturally, both the Devas and the Asuras wanted the amrita for themselves. But the only way to extract the amrita was to churn the sea of milk, just as you would to make butter or cheese. Neither the Devas or Asuras could manage this task on their own so they agreed, just the once, to work together. First, though, they needed to find a rope and a churning stick strong enough for the task. Then the Devas had an idea.

'We'll use this mountain as our churning stick,' they cried, and they pulled up the great mountain, Mount Mandara, which rose huge and steep out of the sea.

The Asuras were not to be outdone. 'We'll use this snake as our rope,' they announced, showing off their find – a gigantic cobra, longer than any other snake

you have ever seen. Indeed, this was no ordinary snake – this was Vasuki, the serpent king.

The Asuras wound the snake around the mountain, coil by coil. Then the Devas took hold of Vasuki's long tail and the Asuras of his huge head, and they began to pull the serpent to and fro with all their might. As they pulled, Mount Mandara began to spin inside the coils of the serpent rope. It spun faster and faster until it was whirling around so fast that the trees on its slopes toppled down and caught fire. Luckily, Lord Indra was close by and quenched the fire with rain from his storm clouds. Even then, the danger was not past. The spinning mountain was so heavy that it began to bore down into the Earth itself, threatening to break the Earth into pieces. So, the great gods sent a gigantic tortoise for the mountain to stand on, and the Earth was saved. The sea of milk began to foam and froth. First it was stirred up into a vast whirlpool of milk, then into thick butter. With their last remaining scraps of strength the Devas and Asuras churned some more, and from the sea of milk came the Sun and the Moon, glittering jewels and other treasures. Finally came the greatest treasure of all, a golden goblet of precious amrita – the elixir of immortality.

The great gods had been watching the proceedings with interest, determined to step in at the last moment to prevent the Asuras from drinking the amrita and becoming more evil than they were already. As soon as the amrita came out of the sea of milk, Lord Vishnu, the preserver, came down to Earth from his vantage point on nearby Mount Meru and snatched the golden goblet away. But before Vishnu could carry the amrita safely back to Mount Meru one of the Asuras, a demon called Rahu, grabbed the goblet and began to drink from it. The Sun and Moon cried out to Vishnu, 'That is the demon, Rahu, most evil of all the Asuras! You must stop him drinking or woe betide us all!'

Fast as a lightning flash, Vishnu acted. Before Rahu could swallow the amrita, Vishnu struck off his head. Rahu's dead body plummeted down towards the Earth but his head rose up into the sky, howling in rage and gnashing its terrible teeth. It could not die – the amrita had reached Rahu's throat and given his head the gift of eternal life.

Then a terrible battle broke out. The Devas and Asuras flew at each other in fury, flinging weapons of thunderbolts, burning mountains and arrows tipped in fire. The battle raged for two days and nights until the Asuras were forced to admit defeat. Thousands of demons and goblins lay dead and dying; thousands more crept away to hide in the pits of the Earth or in the depths of the sea. The great gods divided the amrita amongst themselves and the Devas, and put Mount Mandara back in its rightful place. The only Asura who survived to tell the tale was Rahu's head, forever destined to chase the Moon, its mortal enemy, across the sky. You can see for yourself when Rahu catches the Moon and swallows it, for the Moon wanes in the sky. But the waxing Moon soon reappears as it escapes from Rahu's throat and into the sky again.

HOW SHIVA GOT HIS BLUE THROAT

This is the story of how Lord Shiva, the destroyer, came to have a blue throat.

While the sea of milk was being churned, the great gods – Brahma, Vishnu and Shiva – were watching from Mount Meru. They looked on as the Devas and Asuras pulled Vasuki, the serpent king, to and fro, setting Mount Mandara spinning and the sea foaming and frothing. Of course, the aim of the churning was to extract the amrita, the elixir of eternal life, from the sea. But many other wonderful and beautiful things were cast up, too. Among them were Parijata, the tree of paradise, Varuni, the goddess of wine, and Surabhi, the cow mother. A white horse appeared for Vishnu to ride on, and an elephant for Indra. And still the Devas and Asuras churned to bring forth the amrita.

14

Then there appeared a beautiful goddess. She was more beautiful than any goddess ever seen before, for she was Lakshmi, the goddess of beauty and fortune. Lakshmi sat smiling on an open lotus flower, and she held a lotus flower in one of her four hands. The world was full of praise and love for her. Now, Lakshmi had been born to be Vishnu's wife and the Asuras had no claim to her, much as they wanted her for themselves. In their anger they pulled Vasuki harder and harder and set Mount Mandara spinning faster and faster.

Vasuki suffered greatly. In his pain he opened his jaws, and torrents of blue poison flowed out of his mouth and poured towards the Earth. Had this river of venom reached the land, it would have destroyed the whole world – all the gods, demons, people and animals.

The gods and people alike begged Shiva to save them from such a terrible fate. Quickly, Lord Shiva leapt forward and drank the poison in one go before it touched the Earth. The world was safe but, ever since then, Shiva's throat has been blue where the deadly liquid burned his neck. And this is how he came to be known as 'Nilakantha' – the blue-throated one.

IZANAGI AND IZANAMI

In the Shinto religion of Japan, there is a story that tells how the world was created. In the beginning, the universe was divided into two halves. The top half was heaven. The bottom half was to become the Earth, but it had not yet been given any shape or form. A god, Izanagi, and a goddess, Izanami, were allotted the great task of forming the whirling water into the world that we know today.

Izanagi and Izanami stood on the Floating Bridge of Heaven, which was made of all the colours of the rainbow. They took a long, jewel-covered spear in their hands and with it they stirred the whirling waters below. When they lifted the spear out, a drop of water fell from it and formed the island of Onokoro, the first solid land there had ever been.

Izanagi and Izanami were very pleased with their island. They decided to leave heaven and descend to Earth to live on Onokoro. They built a great palace, with a pillar that reached up to heaven to prop up the roof. Then they got married and had lots of children. The first of their children was born deformed as a punishment from the gods for their past wrongdoings. They called him the leech-child and, placing him in a reed boat, they set him adrift on the sea to drown. But their next children were all healthy. Some became the islands of Japan. Others became the gods of the wind, the trees and the mountains. Then tragedy struck. While she was giving birth to her last child, the god of fire, Izanami was so badly burned that she died. At first, Izanagi was so upset by her death that he could do nothing but weep. From his tears sprang up more gods and goddesses. Then he fell into a terrible rage, picked up his sword and cut off the fire god's head. More gods and goddesses were created from the fire god's blood as it dripped from the sword to the ground.

For a very long time, Izanagi was inconsolable. Without Izanami, life hardly seemed worth living. So he decided to visit Yomi, the Land of the Dead, and try to bring his wife back to life. Izanami met him at the gateway to Yomi, hidden by the shadows and shades of half light. Izanagi begged her to come back with him to their island. She told him that she would go and ask the god of death for his advice, but she warned Izanagi not to try and look at her as she disappeared into the darkness. Izanagi meant to obey her but she was gone for such a long time that he grew impatient. He broke off a tooth from the comb he wore in his hair and lit it to make a torch. Then he followed Izanami inside. And there, in the glowing torchlight, a hideous sight awaited him – Izanami's dead body, rotting and full of worms.

Izanagi ran away as quickly as he could. When he reached the sea, he plunged into the water to wash away the terrible memory of what he had seen. And as he washed, he produced hundreds of gods. From his left eye came Amaterasu, the goddess of the Sun and ruler of heaven; from his right eye came Tsukiyomi, the goddess of the Moon and ruler of the night. From his nose came Susanoo, the god of the sea and of storms and rain. Then Izanagi, his work completed, left the Earth and returned to heaven.

IN THE BEGINNING

In the Christian religion, the story of the seven days of creation and of the appearance on the new Earth of the first man and woman is told in the first book of the Bible – the book of Genesis.

This is how the story goes.

In the beginning, God created the heavens and the Earth. But the Earth was empty and dark, with no shape or form. Then God said, 'Let there be light!' and suddenly, everywhere was bathed in light. God was pleased with what he saw. He separated the light from the darkness and called the light, day, and the darkness, night. And together, day and night became the first day of creation.

On the second day of creation, God began the great task of giving the Earth shape and form. He said, 'Let there be a sky between the Earth and the heavens, to divide one from the other!' And this is how the sky came into being.

On the third day, God created the dry land and the sea. He said, 'Let all the water on the Earth collect and flow together in one place. This shall be the sea. And let the dry land appear from its midst.' No sooner had he spoken, than it was done. The sea stretched out around the land, deep and blue. And the land was carved and folded into high mountains and plunging valleys. The land itself was brown and bare, though not for long. 'Let grass grow on the Earth,' God said, 'and plants bearing seeds, and trees bearing fruit.' And it was so. The Earth bloomed with green grass and plants, and the scent of brightly coloured flowers filled the air. The leaves of countless trees rustled in the breeze, while their branches were bowed low with fruit.

On the fourth day, God said, 'Let there be lights in the sky to divide day from night and to mark the changing of the seasons,

and of the years and days.' And this is what happened. God created two great lights – the Sun to rule the day and the Moon to rule the night. He also made the stars and set them in the sky to shine down on the Earth and lend their brightness to the night sky.

God was pleased with all that he had done. But despite the green grass, the plants and the trees, the Earth was still barren and bare. For there were no creatures anywhere to be seen. So, on the fifth day, God said, 'Let the seas be filled with living creatures, and let birds and insects fly in the skies above the Earth!' And God created the great whales and fish of every colour and size to swim in the seas. Then he created insects and birds, large and small, which fluttered and flew in the air. God blessed all the animals he had made and told them, 'Now, go and multiply in number to fill the seas and skies.'

On the sixth day, God continued this work. He said, 'Let the Earth be filled with animals of every kind – cattle, beasts and creeping things!' And so it was. Creatures great and small, beastly and beautiful, timid and fierce, with tails and without, soon roamed, scuttled and crawled over the whole Earth. Now the Earth was ready for the last of God's creations – human beings. God created people in his own image, to rule over the Earth and everything that moves on it, the fish in the sea, the birds in the sky and all the beasts on the land. He picked up two handfuls of dust and from them he created a man and a woman, called Adam and Eve. As he breathed life into their bodies, God said to Adam and Eve, 'Go into the world and fill the Earth with your children and your children's children. I have given you power over all the animals on the Earth and provided you with plants, seeds and fruits for food.' And the man and the woman did as God had told them. Then the rain came down, giving the animals water to drink and the plants water to grow.

On the seventh day of creation, the sea, the sky and the land were finished and filled with life. God rested from his work, pleased with what he could see all about him. And every seventh day after this one has been kept as a holy day of rest, because this is the day on which God rested after he created the world.

OLD SPIDER AND THE GIANT CLAMSHELL

The Polynesian island of Nauru in the Pacific Ocean has its very own story of creation.

At the beginning of time there was nothing but sea, all around and about. Above the sea there soared a huge spider, called Old Spider. One day, Old Spider found a giant clamshell. She picked it up and tapped it with two of her arms. The shell sounded hollow and she decided that it must be empty. But still she twisted and turned it this way and that to find a way of prising it open. But she couldn't find a single chink or opening. So she spoke a magic charm which pulled the two halves of the shell apart just wide enough for her to slip inside.

It was dark, very dark, inside the clamshell. Old Spider couldn't see a thing because the Sun and the Moon did not exist yet. Nor was there enough room for Old Spider to stand up. She hunted about and finally she found a tiny snail. She tucked it under one arm to give it magic powers, then lay down and slept for three days and three nights. Then she let the little snail go. Once again, she hunted about until she found another snail, a bit bigger than the first. She tucked it under another arm to give it magic powers, then lay down and slept for three days and three nights. Then she let the big snail go.

Old Spider said to the first snail, 'Can you push these shells a little further apart so that we have room to stand up?'

'Yes,' said the snail, 'I can.' And it pushed the shells a little further apart.

Then Old Spider picked up the little snail and placed it very carefully in the west of the shell and it became the Moon. By the pale light given off by the Moon, Old Spider caught sight of a large caterpillar sitting inside the shell.

'Can you push these shells further apart still?' Old Spider asked the caterpillar.

'Yes,' the caterpillar replied, 'I can.' And it pushed the shells with all its might. It pushed so hard that salty sweat dripped from its body and formed a pool in the bottom half of the clamshell. The shell became the Earth and the salty sweat the salty sea. A second time the caterpillar pushed, until the top half of the shell was as high as it would go. This half of the shell became the sky. Then, all its strength gone, the caterpillar curled up and died of exhaustion.

Old Spider picked up the big snail, placed it in the sky and it became the Sun. And this is how the world began.

MEN, MONKEYS AND MUKULU

In Africa, some people believe in a bad spirit, called Minepa, and a good spirit, called Mukulu. This is the story of how Mukulu created the first man and the first woman.

Mukulu dug two deep holes in the dusty ground. From one of the holes, a man appeared. From the other, a woman. Mukulu, the good spirit, gave them land to farm, a pick and an axe, plates, a cooking pot and some grain to sow. He told them to prepare the land and sow their grain, to build themselves a house and make themselves a fire for cooking their food. But the man and woman took no notice of what Mukulu said. They neglected their land, ate their food raw, made the pot dirty and cracked and smashed the plates. Then they ran away into the forest and hid.

Mukulu was angry that the man and woman had disobeyed him. He, too, went into the forest and found a male and a female monkey. He provided them with land to farm, a pick and axe, plates, a cooking pot

and some grain to sow. And he gave them exactly the same instructions as he had given the man and the woman. Unlike the people, the monkeys did what Mukulu had told them. They tilled the land, sowed the grain, built themselves a hut and cooked their food on a fire. Mukulu was very pleased with them. So pleased, in fact, that he cut off their tails and stuck them on to the man and woman.

'Be people!' he said to the monkeys.

'Be monkeys!' he said to the people.

THE EARTH DIVER

The North American Indian peoples have many myths and legends about the world around them and how it came to be. The Cheyenne story of creation goes like this.

In the beginning, the Great Spirit, Maheo, created the water and all the creatures that lived in it. For a time, all was well. The birds were content to fly above the water and the fish to swim in its depths. But the day came when the birds grew tired of flying. They began to take it in turns to dive into the sea to look for land where they might rest and build their nests. One by one they dived, but they failed to find any land. Finally, the coot made its last dive. When it came to the surface again it was holding a little ball of mud in its beak. It dropped the mud into Maheo's hand. Now, Maheo possessed great powers. He kneaded and rolled the ball of mud in his hands and, as he did so, the ball of mud grew bigger. It grew so big, in fact, that the only creature strong enough to carry it was old Grandmother Turtle. The mud continued to grow on her broad, strong back and formed the land the birds had been looking for.

YIN, YANG AND THE COSMIC EGG

The ancient Chinese story of creation begins with two forces – Yin, the power of darkness and shadow, and Yang, the power of sunshine and light. Yin and Yang had a child, a god called Pan Gu, and it was he who formed the world as we know it.

Pan Gu was born inside a huge egg. Inside the egg, everything was dark. For eighteen thousand years, Pan Gu lived in the darkness of the egg, growing steadily bigger. Finally, he grew so big that the egg could not hold him. Cracks appeared in its shell – wider and wider until the egg split open. The clear, light parts of the egg floated upwards to form the heavens. The dark, heavy parts of the egg sank downwards to form the Earth.

Then Pan Gu broke free of the egg and stood up, straight and tall. To stop the heavens and Earth merging into one again he grew taller still and, each day, pushed them further apart. Another eighteen thousand years passed in this way. Then, Pan Gu, wearied by his great work, lay down and died. His breath formed the clouds and wind, his rumbling voice became the thunder. His right eye became the Moon and his left eye the Sun. His hair and his whiskers became the stars in the sky. The rain and dew formed from his sweat, and the rivers, mountains, plants and trees, rocks and precious gems were also created from his body.

INCA ANCESTORS

The powerful Inca empire ruled over large parts of South America from the 12th to the 15th century AD. The natural world around the Incas was dominated by the Andes Mountains, and mountains, considered sacred places, play an important part in many Inca myths and legends. The Incas believed that their ancestors came from the mountains near Lake Titicaca. This is the story the Incas told of their arrival in the world.

The first people were created by the god, Viracocha. He made their bodies out of clay and painted clothes on them. Then he breathed life into them and told them to go down to Earth to the shelter of caves, mountains and lakes. The world was still in darkness. Viracocha ordered the Sun, the Moon and the stars to rise up from the Island of the Sun in Lake Titicaca and light up the world. At the first sunrise, Viracocha called on the Incas. He told them to emerge as rulers and conquerors of the world.

So the Incas went down into the Earth and emerged from three caves in the mountainside. There were six of them in all, three brothers and three sisters, all dressed in fine woollen clothes. One of the brothers was much stronger than the others. He began to hurl stones into the distant land to form mountains and valleys. The others were jealous of his strength so they tricked him into going back into the cave, telling him tales of the sacred llama and the golden goblet he would find there. The brother couldn't resist. But no sooner was he inside the cave than his brothers and sisters sealed it behind him.

Some time later, the brother managed to escape and went to live on top of a high mountain. He summoned his brothers and sisters to him, telling them that, from now on, they must always wear earrings made of the purest gold to show their royal status. Then he turned himself and another brother into stone. The third, and last, brother survived. He went on to found the city of Cuzco, the glorious capital of the Inca empire.

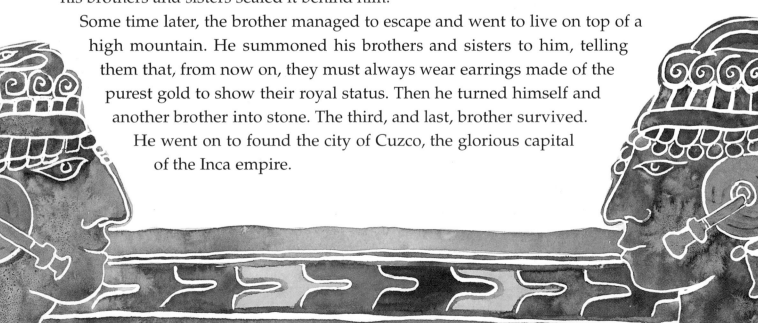

EA, ZIUSDRA AND THE GREAT FLOOD

Many religions have stories about a great flood sent by the gods to punish human beings for their wickedness. In these stories, a few people and animals survive the flood by living aboard a huge boat, called an ark. Many of the stories are very similar to each other. In the Christian Bible, you can read about Noah and the ark; in the Muslim Koran, about the ark built by the prophet, Nuh. This story comes from the ancient religion of Babylon.

Long ago, in the land called Babylon that lay between the mighty rivers Tigris and Euphrates, the people worshipped many gods. One day, the gods assembled on the river bank to debate the fate of humankind, for people had become wicked and lazy. They were cruel, warlike, and greedy for money and riches. They remembered the wise words and commandments of the gods, but they chose to ignore them. They had to be soundly punished.

'What shall we do about these people?' asked the great god, Anu. 'It makes me sad to see them.'

'Sad?' boomed Enlil, the god of storms and hurricanes. 'Sad? It makes me angry, after all we've done for them. I vote we send a great flood to drown the whole Earth and everything that lives on it. Get rid of the lot of them, once and for all!'

The other gods nodded their approval. But Ea, the god of wisdom and knowledge, took pity on the people of the Earth, and he decided to try and help them. First, he had to persuade the gods to spare one man, called Ziusdra, whom Ea knew to be good, kind and law-abiding. It wasn't an easy task.

'I give you my word,' pleaded Ea. 'This man, Ziusdra, is a good man. Surely we can spare him and his family, at least?'

'Oh no,' replied Enlil. 'No, no, no! They must all die. We can't start making exceptions now. And don't try to warn them, Ea. We must keep our plan secret.'

Ea's heart sank. What should he do? He couldn't stand by and watch good people like Ziusdra die. But he couldn't deliberately disobey the other gods either. Eventually, after many days spent in thought, he came up with a plan.

That night, Ea went to the house where Ziusdra lived. Now, Ea knew that he must not warn Ziusdra directly. So he whispered his warning to the walls of the house, in the hope that Ziusdra would overhear.

'Sturdy walls,' began Ea, in a low voice, 'listen carefully to what I say. The gods are tired of people's sinful ways and have vowed to punish them. They will send a mighty flood to cover the land and drown every living thing on the Earth. Nothing will escape the waters of the flood unless Ziusdra does what I tell him.'

Inside the house, Ziusdra was listening intently – Ea's plan was working.

'Ziusdra must tear down his house and build a great boat from the timbers and reeds. He should take his wife and family, his loyal servants and two of every kind of animal and bird that lives on Earth. Sturdy walls,' Ea continued, 'be sure to heed these words! Unless Ziusdra does as I say, the whole Earth is doomed.'

So Ziusdra set to work to build a great boat, just as Ea had ordered him to. His wife, his family and his loyal servants all helped, working day and night. The boat was huge – as big as a palace, with six decks piled one on top of the other, and a hundred cabins inside. When it was finished Ziusdra collected two of every kind of animal and bird that lived on the Earth – eagles and ants, elephants and antelopes, snakes, tigers and butterflies. From the largest to the smallest they came, two by two, and soon the boat was full. And just as the last pair of animals boarded the boat, the rain began to fall as Ea had said it would.

The rain was like nothing ever seen before. The sky was black with rainclouds – even during the daytime. Thunder rumbled and roared; great flashes of lightning streaked across the sky. The people were terrified and hid in their houses – but in vain. Rivers burst their banks and still the rain came, covering the land and drowning everything that lived on the Earth. For six days and nights the storm raged as if it would never stop. Even the gods were afraid. The only survivors on the whole of the Earth were the people, animals and birds safe on Ziusdra's boat.

On the seventh day, the storm died down. The wind grew still and the sea became calm. Ziusdra looked at the devastation all about him and tears came to his eyes. But he didn't forget to pray to Ea.

'Oh Ea, great god, I thank you for sparing my family and myself. Thanks to you there will still be animals and birds to roam and fly about the Earth.'

Meanwhile, Ziusdra's boat had come to rest on the summit of a mighty mountain, the only land to have emerged from the waves. Then Ziusdra let loose a jet-black raven.

'Fly, beautiful raven, fly as fast as you can,' Ziusdra said. 'Find dry land where we can spend our days and build a new world.'

The raven flew away and did not come back.

Ziusdra knew that the raven had found dry land and he set off to follow in his boat. He found the raven in a lush green valley, with trees all around and a rippling stream. Ziusdra flung open the doors of the boat and out came the animals and birds, two by two, of every kind. Last of all came Ziusdra with his wife, his family and his loyal servants, their hearts filled with joy. And they all lived happily in the valley, to the end of their days.

HOW THE FISH SAVED MANU

At the very beginning of creation, so the Hindu story says, there lived a man called Manu, the first man on Earth. Manu was a good and holy man. He meditated every day, and every day he prayed to the gods and bathed in the river to wash away his sins.

One day, as Manu was bathing in the river, he scooped up a tiny fish in his hands.

'If you look after me,' the fish said to Manu, 'I will save your life.'

'But why does my life need saving?' Manu asked, puzzled. 'I didn't know it was in danger.'

'The gods are angry,' the fish explained. 'They are sending a great flood to destroy the Earth and everything that lives on it. The waters will wipe away all the evil that there is on Earth, then the gods will start all over again.'

'Very well,' said Manu, greatly alarmed at this news. 'Then please tell me how I should look after you.'

'As long as I'm so very small,' the fish began, 'my days are numbered. For a bigger fish is sure to gobble me up sooner or later. Put me into a pot, so I can grow. And when I grow too big for the pot, put me into a tank, then into a lake – and then into the sacred River Ganges.'

Manu put the little fish into a pot where it grew until the pot could no longer hold it. So Manu put it into a tank, then into a lake and, when it grew too big even for the lake, he put it into the sacred River Ganges. And still the fish grew until it was so squashed and squeezed between the river banks that it could hardly breathe.

'Take me down to the sea,' it gasped. 'It is the only place on Earth big enough to hold me.'

So Manu hauled the gigantic fish down to the sea and threw it into the water, with a huge splash.

The fish swam joyfully through the waves, diving and leaping in the vast expanse of the ocean. Then it said to Manu, 'I owe you a favour, Manu, for saving my life. As I have said, the gods will soon send a great flood to destroy the Earth. You must build a ship and collect on it one of every living thing on Earth, every plant, animal and bird, god and demon. Unless you save them, they will perish. And when the waters begin to rise, get into your ship and I will save you.'

Manu did exactly what the fish told him. From every corner of the Earth, he collected plants, animals and birds, gods and demons and brought them all to his ship. And when the rain began and thunder and lightning engulfed the sky, Manu got into the ship as the fish had said. Then, the fish appeared.

'You have done well, Manu,' it said. 'I knew I could count on you. Now, tie the ship's rope to my tail and I will tow you to safety.'

Manu tied the rope to the fish's tail and the fish pulled the ship across the sea to a high mountain, the top of which could just be seen above the water.

'You will be safe here,' said the fish. 'Tie your ship to that tree and wait for the water to subside. But don't get caught high and dry. Make sure you loosen the rope as the water falls.' Then the fish turned and began to swim away. Before it disappeared, Manu shouted after it,

'But how did you know all this would happen? What sort of fish are you?'

'A strange fish indeed,' the fish replied. 'I am Lord Vishnu, the world's creator. And my task was to save you from the flood.' And then it swam away.

For twelve long years the rain came down and Manu stayed on the mountainside. At last, the rain stopped and the water subsided. Manu loosened the rope to lower the ship. Soon there was enough dry land to open the doors of the ship and let out the plants, animals and birds, and the gods and demons. And the world was filled with life again, thanks to Manu and the fish.

31

THE LIE AND EVIL ENTER THE ARK

This story, from the Jewish religion, is part of the tale of Noah who, like Ziusdra, was told by God to build an ark to escape from the great flood.

When Noah began to build his ark, people thought he was mad. They laughed and jeered at him while he worked.

'Haven't you noticed, Noah,' they sniggered, 'that there isn't any water for your precious boat to float in? Ha, ha, ha!'

Noah took no notice of their jibes. God had warned him that a mighty flood would soon sweep over the Earth. He had instructed Noah to build a great boat and gather on board his family and two of every kind of animal, bird and reptile that walked or flew or swam on the Earth. Every other living thing – man, woman and beast – would be drowned by the waters of the flood. So Noah continued in his task, oblivious to the sarcastic remarks and secure in the knowledge that he was following God's commandments.

One day, when the ark was almost finished and it was nearly time for the animals to come on board, the Lie appeared by Noah's side.

'Oh Noah,' the Lie said, in a wheedling voice, 'they say that the rains are coming and we'll all be drowned. Could you find room for me on your ark? I'm only quite small, after all.'

Noah had an uneasy feeling about the Lie. So, in reply, he said,
'No, there's um, er, there's … No, I'm sorry, but there it is.'
But the Lie wasn't going to be put off that easily.
'Oh, please, Noah,' he whined. 'Pleeeeease.'

Noah was getting flustered. He couldn't think of a good enough excuse to prevent the Lie from coming aboard. After all, he'd invited every other kind of living thing. But he just didn't like the look of the Lie. Then he had a brainwave.

'You can't come on your own,' Noah said. 'Everyone else is coming in pairs.'

'No problem,' said the Lie, 'I'll find someone.' And off he ran to find a partner.

The Lie asked every animal, bird and reptile that he met to join him on the ark, but they all refused and ran away. He was wicked and completely untrustworthy, and nobody wanted to know him. Time was running out for the Lie when, one day, as even the Lie was beginning to despair, he met the girl of his dreams. Her name was Evil. She was every bit as wicked and untrustworthy as he was. The Lie explained his dilemma and then he asked Evil if she would marry him.

Evil didn't even stop to think. 'Yes,' she said, immediately. So the Lie and Evil got married and raced back to the ark. They arrived just as Noah was about to shut the wooden doors.

'Noah, oh Noah,' whined the Lie, 'let me introduce you to my wife! The two of us would like to come on board. Any objections?'

There was nothing Noah could do. With great reluctance, he pushed back the doors and the Lie and Evil entered the ark.

For forty days and nights the rain came down and covered the Earth in water. The ark and its passengers, the Lie and Evil amongst them, bobbed safely up and down on the waves. At last, the storm died down and the rain stopped. The ark came to rest on dry land and Noah opened the doors and let down the gangplank. Two by two the animals, birds and reptiles left the ark. Last of all, the Lie and Evil came out of the ark and followed the animals on to the land.

God spoke to the animals and said, 'Go to all four corners of the Earth. Multiply and fill the land, the sea and the sky with life.'

And this they did. They roamed far and wide, and soon the world was filled with their children and grandchildren. But the Lie and Evil also roamed far and wide, and soon their children and grandchildren, lies and evils every one, filled the world too. And so the sin and wickedness that God had sent the great flood to destroy appeared on the Earth once again.

FIRE, ICE AND FLOOD

According to a story told by the Hopi Indians of North America, there have been various worlds before this one and each has been destroyed by a different disaster. The first world was burnt to cinders by a terrible fire, as punishment for people's evil ways. The second world came to an end when the Earth toppled off its axis and everything, land and sea, became covered in ice. A great flood devastated the third world. The world in which we live is the fourth world. Its fate depends on how well its inhabitants behave and how far they obey the wishes of the gods.

The Aztecs, who lived in Central America more than four hundred years ago, had a similar legend. They believed that the first world had been eaten by jaguars; the second blown apart by a great hurricane; the third devastated by fire and the fourth by flood. The fifth world (the one we live in) is fated to be destroyed by a massive earthquake.

THE GREAT BRONZE BUDDHA AND THE WHALE

Long ago, in Japan, there lived a huge whale. He was not only bigger than any other whale; he was bigger than any other creature there had ever been. And he was very proud of the fact. The whale lived far down in the dark depths of the sea. When he needed some air, he rose to the surface and spouted a tall fountain of water from the blowhole on the top of his head. Then his vast, grey body crashed back down into the water, sending a spread of ripples scurrying across the sea.

The fish, crabs, turtles and all the other animals in the sea were afraid of the whale because of his great size. They kept as far away from him as possible and swam in the other direction as fast as they could whenever they saw him coming. Fortunately for them, he was easy to spot. The whale was quite happy about the commotion he caused. In fact, he was rather flattered. After all, wasn't he the biggest animal that had ever lived? This was just proof that nothing could match him in size – or so he liked to believe.

The only creature who was not afraid of the whale was a tiny sprat, about as long as your little finger. One day, the sprat swam right up to the whale's head and looked him straight in the eye (well, almost). In the bravest voice it could muster, the sprat spoke to the whale.

'Master Whale,' the sprat said, 'Master Whale, I've just heard a wonderful thing which might be of interest to you.'

'I'm listening, little sprat,' boomed the whale. 'What exactly is it that you've heard?'

'I was swimming around the fishermen's boat and I overheard them talking.'

'Yes, and what did you hear?' said the whale, beginning to lose patience ever so slightly.

'They were talking about the great bronze Buddha on the island of Kamakura,' the sprat burbled, wondering if what it was doing was altogether sensible and weighing up its chances of escaping alive. 'They said that it was the biggest thing in the whole world.'

'Hah!' said the whale, scornfully. 'That's because they have never seen me!'

'No, Master Whale,' the sprat replied. 'But they have been to Kamakura and they have seen the great bronze Buddha.'

The whale said nothing. He closed his eyes and thought, deeply. He was silent for such a long time that the sprat grew rather nervous. Then the whale opened his eyes, sighed, and said, 'And just how big is this great bronze Buddha supposed to be?'

'The Buddha's face is three metres long, and each of his thumbs measures a metre round,' the sprat replied. 'The Buddha's body, sitting down, is seventeen metres tall and thirty-three metres right around.'

'Well, well,' the whale said, in a smug voice.

'This Buddha of yours is certainly large. But not as large as I am. After all, nothing is as large as I am.'

'You're probably right,' said the sprat. 'But you've never been measured!'

That did it. The whale was furious. He told the sprat to go away while it still had the chance. It didn't need telling twice.

When he was alone, the whale thought about what the sprat had said. He wanted to see the Buddha for himself but he was worried. All his life he'd simply assumed that he was bigger than anything else in the world. What if the fishermen had been telling the truth and the Buddha was bigger? He began to regret sending the sprat away. He should have asked it some more questions.

Some days later, he got his chance. The sprat plucked up its courage again and swam back to the whale.

'Master Whale,' it said, in a trembling voice. 'I've heard some more about the great bronze Buddha.'

'Spit it out then,' said the whale.

'I swam to the island of Kamakura,' the sprat told him, 'and there I met a rat who was trembling with fear.'

'And?' demanded the whale.

'And,' said the sprat, 'the reason he was frightened was because of the great bronze Buddha's size! He'd crept into the temple where the Buddha sits and run all the way around him. And all the way around him measures five thousand paces!'

'Five thousand paces!' the whale roared, in a voice that could be heard on the other side of the ocean. 'Are you sure?'

The sprat didn't wait to be sure. It swam away from the whale as fast and as far as it could and hid.

Meanwhile, the whale had made up his mind. He decided to visit the island of Kamakura to see the great bronze Buddha for himself. He swam all day and all night to reach the island. To get to the temple where the Buddha sat, the whale had to come out of the water and walk on dry land for the first time in his life. As he approached the temple door he heard a deep voice, musical as a chiming bell, saying, 'Who is there?'

'It is I, the whale, the biggest creature in the whole wide world,' the whale replied, in his most important voice.

'Come inside,' the musical voice said.

'No!' the whale said. 'You come out!'

There followed a sound like the crash of thunder and a huge figure appeared in the temple doorway. The great bronze Buddha had risen to his feet.

'Why do you wish to see me?' asked the Buddha.

'I wanted to find out the truth,' the whale replied. 'The fishermen said you were bigger than I am, and I wanted to see if they were right.'

The Buddha smiled, a smile filled with kindliness and peacefulness. He called to the priest who was sleeping in the temple. Rubbing his eyes, the saffron-robed priest came out. When he saw the two figures – the great bronze Buddha and the whale – he fell to his knees and touched the Buddha's feet in awe.

'Don't be afraid,' the Buddha told him. 'There's something I want you to do for me. I want you to measure us both – me and my friend, the whale.'

The priest rose to his feet. First, he measured the whale. Then he measured the great bronze Buddha. It was no mean task. It took the priest a day and a night to measure them both.

At last, he said, 'I have measured you both, Lord Buddha, and you both measure exactly the same.'

The great bronze Buddha smiled again.

'I hope you'll agree, my friend, that this is the fairest result we could hope for,' he said to the whale. 'I am the biggest thing on all the land and you are the biggest thing in all the sea.'

'I do agree, most certainly,' the whale replied. And he set off back to the sea, as happy as could be.

THE VALLEY OF THE ANTS

This story comes from the Muslim holy book, the Koran. It is one of many stories that show how Allah is merciful to even the smallest of his creatures.

Long ago, the ants lived in their own peaceful valley. They worked happily together, always busy finding food, building or repairing their nests and looking after their young. A large and powerful queen ant ruled over them. The ants were proud of the way they lived. They never quarrelled or fought amongst themselves, and they always helped each other if help was needed. The Valley of the Ants was the finest home in the world.

One day, when the ants were hard at work, they heard a terrible noise in the distance. It could have been the rumble of thunder, except that the sky was clear and blue. It could have been the roar of a tornado, except that the day was quite still, without the slightest breeze.

'Whatever is that noise?' the ants asked each other, in the deepest puzzlement. But nobody knew the answer.

As they listened, the sound came closer and closer and grew louder and louder. Still, none of the ants could say what it was. All they knew was that it was the most frightening noise they had ever heard. The ants began to dash for cover, scuttling and scurrying hither and thither in search of a hole or a crack in a rock to give them shelter.

So great was the commotion that it brought the queen ant hurrying out of her royal chamber. She was amazed to see all the ants rushing about in panic, and she asked one of them what was going on.

'Your Majesty,' the ant stuttered, 'Your Majesty, there's a terrible noise and it's coming this way, right into our valley. Oh, what shall we do? What shall we do?'

The queen ant thought quickly. She summoned the ants together and told them to gather up as much food as they could and to stay close to their nests. And she told them not to panic. Then the queen climbed to the top of the tallest nest and peered down the valley in the direction of the terrible noise. A great grey shape was coming closer and closer. At last, the queen could make out what it was – a huge and magnificent army of soldiers

on foot and on horseback, led by the great prophet, Sulaiman (Solomon). The noise the ants could hear was the stomp, stomp, stomp of the army's marching feet. There was no time to lose.

'The prophet Sulaiman and his army are coming into our valley,' the queen told the ants. 'That is the noise you can hear. Now go to your nests, as quickly as you can, to avoid being crushed. We are so small, the soldiers might not see us in time.'

But Sulaiman heard the queen's words and he understood them, for Allah had taught his prophet the language of the birds and of all the other animals. He smiled gently and ordered his mighty army to stop marching. The terrible noise stopped with them. Sulaiman instructed his soldiers to tread very carefully as they moved through the valley so that they would not step on any of the ants. And, truth to tell, so light were their steps, that not a single ant was killed.

That night, when the army had passed by and gone on its way, peace and quiet returned to the Valley of the Ants. But the ants never forgot Sulaiman, the great and merciful prophet who could understand the language even of Allah's smallest creatures.

HANUMAN AND THE SEARCH FOR SITA

In India, there was once a prince called Rama who was brave, handsome and good. He was married to a gentle and beautiful princess called Sita. One day, while Rama and Sita were walking in the forest, Sita vanished. Rama was heartbroken, for he loved Sita dearly.

'I can think of only one person who would steal my wife,' Rama cried, 'and that is Ravana, the demon king. He must have kidnapped her.' And he was right. For Ravana, the ten-headed, twenty-armed king of the demons, had been told that if he married Sita he would become ruler of all the world.

In his despair, Rama turned to his trusty friend, Hanuman, for help. Hanuman was a monkey, son of the god of the wind and leader of the monkey king's mighty army. He had many magical powers.

'My friend, I need you to find Sita, so that we can plan how to rescue her,' Rama told Hanuman.

So Hanuman set off with his army of monkeys from all four corners of the Earth. The monkeys searched high and low, village and city, forest and desert, but Sita was nowhere to be found. Then Hanuman flew right down to the southernmost tip of India, at the ocean's edge. There he met the vulture king.

'I am looking for Sita, wife of Lord Rama,' Hanuman said. 'Have you seen her on your travels?'

'Indeed, I have,' replied the vulture king. 'The evil Ravana carried her off in his chariot, over the ocean to his palace on the island of Lanka. Look over there at that dot in the distance – that is Lanka.'

Hanuman looked. The island was too far away for an ordinary monkey to jump across to it. But Hanuman was no ordinary monkey – his father was the god of the wind. So, he climbed to the top of the highest cliff and with a mighty leap, soared through the clouds and right across the ocean to Lanka. From the shore, Hanuman could see Ravana's great city. The city walls were high and imposing. The city gates were guarded by demon soldiers. Hanuman waited for nightfall before he dared to enter the city. Then, he made himself as small as an ant and crept inside.

He made his way towards Ravana's palace, a magnificent building of white marble and gold which glistened and glittered in the moonlight. He crept through the palace, down corridor after corridor, and through courtyard after courtyard. In one room he caught sight of Ravana's warrior son, Indrajit, sprawled across his bed in his armour. In another room he saw Ravana himself, his ten hideous heads all fast asleep. But Sita was nowhere to be found.

At last, Hanuman found himself in a splendid orchard. There he saw Sita, looking pale and tired, surrounded by demon guards. Hanuman crept silently up to her and whispered in her ear, 'Oh Princess Sita, I am glad to have found you. Rama has sent me. Here is his ring to prove that I am telling you the truth.'

Sita was overjoyed. She gave Hanuman a precious jewel to take back to Rama, together with all her love. However, before Hanuman left the palace he decided to cause a spot of mischief. He grew as big as a giant and began uprooting the trees in the orchard and tossing them over the walls. The terrified guards ran to wake Ravana. The demon king was not best pleased and he sent soldiers to capture Hanuman, but Hanuman killed them all with a giant club. Then Ravana sent his son, Indrajit, to defeat the monkey. There followed a terrible fight during which Indrajit hit Hanuman with one of his magical arrows and ensnared him in its power. Then Hanuman was tied up with ropes of living snakes and taken to Ravana.

Ravana sat on his jewel-encrusted throne, tapping several of his twenty arms in turn and shaking his ten heads in fury.

'To what do I owe this honour, monkey?' asked the demon king, sarcastically.

'I have come as a messenger from Rama,' Hanuman replied, 'to tell you to return Sita to her rightful home. And no-one disobeys Lord Rama.'

'Is that right?' shrieked Ravana, flying into a rage. 'Well, I've got news for you! You have come as a messenger so I cannot kill you. But I have a much better punishment in store for you – just you wait.'

And, knowing how much monkeys prize their tails, Ravana ordered his guards to set fire to Hanuman's tail. In the orchard, Sita heard the commotion. She prayed to Agni, god of fire, to spare Hanuman. Her prayers were answered. Although Hanuman's tail blazed brightly, he felt no pain and not a hair on his body was singed. Then Hanuman slipped out of the snake ropes and ran from the palace and into the city. As he went, he swished his tail this way and that setting fire first to the palace itself, then to the wooden houses of the city. Confusion and panic reigned everywhere.

When Hanuman reached the ocean, he dipped his tail into the water to put out the flames. Then, he climbed to the top of a mountain and, with another mighty leap, jumped across the ocean, back to India and to Rama. He told Rama that Sita had been found and gave him her precious jewel as proof. Now it was up to Rama to rescue her, for only he could do so.

THE HARE AND THE EARTHQUAKE

There are many stories about how the Buddha has appeared as an animal in times of trouble. This is what happened when the Buddha took on the disguise of a lion.

Once upon a time, a hare lived under a wood-apple tree in a forest by the sea. One day, as he was sitting under his tree, the hare had a terrible thought:

'What if the Earth fell to pieces? What would become of me then?'

At that very moment, a huge, ripe wood-apple fell from the tree and landed with a gigantic thud on the ground right behind the hare. The hare nearly jumped out of his skin. His worst fears had come true. The Earth was falling to pieces right around his ears. So he took to his heels and ran.

As he ran, another hare asked him what was the matter.

'The Earth is falling to pieces!' cried the first hare. 'Run for your life!' And the second hare ran after him. Soon the hare was being followed by a hundred other hares, not to mention a deer, a wild boar, a buffalo and a rhinoceros. Before long, a tiger, an antelope and an elephant had joined the throng of animals as they ran towards the sea.

Then a great lion appeared in front of them.

'Whatever is the matter?' the lion asked. 'Where are you all going?'

'The Earth is falling to pieces!' cried the animals. 'The hare told us! Run, run for your life!'

The lion was puzzled.

'There hasn't been an earthquake,' he thought. 'They must have heard some other noise. If I don't act quickly, they will all run into the sea and drown.'

So he bounded to the front of the throng of animals and roared his mighty roar, once, twice, then a third time, to get their attention. The animals stopped in their tracks. When a lion roared, you had to obey.

'Now,' said the lion, calmly. 'Why are you running away?'

'The Earth is falling to pieces,' came the reply.

'Has anyone seen this happening?' asked the lion.

'The elephants have,' they said.

But the elephants said the tigers had, and the tigers said the deer had, and the deer said the buffalo had, and the buffalo said it was the hares. And the hares pointed to the very first hare who had started the whole thing off.

'And where exactly did you see the Earth falling to pieces?' asked the lion.

'Well, sir,' began the hare, 'I was sitting at home, under a wood-apple tree in the forest near the sea, when I heard a terrible crash right behind me. Then I ran away as fast as I could.'

'So that's it,' thought the lion, with relief. 'A wood-apple must have fallen from the tree and crashed to the ground. That's what he heard!'

The lion told the animals that he was taking the hare to investigate the scene of the earthquake, and that they were all to wait until he came back. With the hare on his back, the lion ran to the forest near the sea, as fast as the wind. In the forest, the hare pointed to the wood-apple tree but he didn't dare go near it. The lion walked round the tree and saw the spot where the wood-apple fruit had crashed to the ground. Then he told the hare to hop on his back again and they hurried back to the animals. The lion explained what had happened and told the animals that it was now quite safe for them to return home.

And that is how the Buddha, in the guise of a lion, saved all the animals from plunging into the sea.

THE STORY OF MARYAM'S SON

There was once a young girl called Maryam. She was good, pretty and pure, and she was Allah's chosen one. Every day, Maryam went to the temple and asked Allah to watch over her and help her lead a good life. And Allah answered her prayers and protected her from harm.

One day, Maryam was worshipping in the temple when, suddenly, a young man appeared as if from nowhere. Maryam was terrified but something stopped her from running away. Her voice trembled as she pleaded, 'Please don't hurt me. Allah is watching over me.'

'Don't be afraid, Maryam,' the young man replied, with a smile. 'I have been sent by Allah with a message for you. It's about your son, who will be called Messiah and who will be very great.'

In amazement, Maryam realized that this was no ordinary young man. It was the angel, Jibril.

'How can I have a son?' she asked him, greatly puzzled. 'I am not yet married.'

'This will be Allah's son,' was Jibril's reply, 'the son of God.' Then he was gone.

Maryam tried hard to feel glad at the news she had received. After all, she had been chosen to have Allah's son. But the more she thought about it, the more unhappy it made her. It wouldn't take long for people to start gossiping about her if she had a baby and no husband. And what would her family say?

As the days went by, Maryam felt more and more miserable. What should she do? She couldn't stay and have her baby at home, that was certain. So, one night, she secretly packed her bag and went to a small village far away where nobody knew her. There she had her baby, in the shade of a tree, while the angel Jibril watched over her. The baby was called Messiah, which means Maryam's son.

Maryam looked down at her tiny, newborn son, tears pricking at her eyes as she

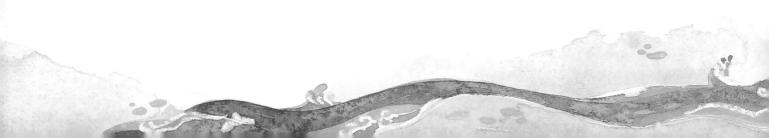

thought of all the cruel things people would say if they knew about him.

'Allah will look after you,' Jibril told her, reading her thoughts. 'Don't be frightened. Look, he has sent cool water to refresh you.'

And water began to flow out of the ground under Maryam's feet.

Then Jibril said, 'Now give the branch of that old palm tree a good shake.'

Maryam did so, and found her hands full of delicious fruit. Then Jibril went away. Maryam ate some of the fruit and drank some of the water. She soon felt stronger and braver and, with her baby in her arms, she set off on the journey home. Her family were astonished to see her. At first, no-one said a word. Then they all started shouting and screaming at once.

'Oh, Maryam, you wicked girl!'

'You've disgraced the whole family!'

'And you were always so good!'

Maryam said nothing. There was no point – they wouldn't listen to anything she had to say. Instead, she pointed to her baby. He would speak for her.

'Have you gone mad, Maryam?' her family sneered. 'A baby can't tell us where he comes from!'

But they were wrong.

'Allah has sent me,' the baby told them, as they stared in amazement, 'to be his servant and prophet. My mother was chosen by Allah.'

Then they understood.

THE FIRST CHRISTMAS

On 25 December each year, Christians all over the world celebrate the birth of Jesus Christ which took place in Bethlehem some two thousand years ago. The beginning of this story is very similar to the story of Maryam.

There was once a young woman called Mary who lived in the city of Nazareth. She was engaged to be married to a man called Joseph, the local carpenter. One day, an astonishing thing happened. A golden light filled Mary's house, and out of the light stepped the angel Gabriel.

'Don't be afraid, Mary,' Gabriel said. 'The Lord has sent me with a special message. He has chosen you to have his son, a baby boy called Jesus who shall save the world from evil and sin.'

And with that, the angel disappeared, leaving Mary to ponder his news. The angel Gabriel visited Joseph, too, and explained everything to him. Not very long after this, Mary and Joseph were married and settled down to live happily ever after.

Some months later, the Roman government, which ruled at the time, passed a decree that everyone should return to the place of their birth to be counted and taxed. Mary and Joseph had to travel to Bethlehem, where Joseph had been born. The road was rocky and bumpy, and at night the travellers slept on the ground by the wayside with a small fire for warmth and to keep wild beasts at bay. At last, Joseph saw Bethlehem in the distance.

'Not much further now,' he told Mary. She sighed with relief. Her baby would be born very soon now.

When they reached the town, the streets were crowded with travellers like themselves, all looking for somewhere to stay. Every inn was full to the brim.

'No vacancies,' shouted one innkeeper.

'You'll be lucky,' cried another.

'There's no room in the inn,' said another, taking pity on them. 'But you could sleep in the stable out the back. It's nice and warm, and the straw's clean.'

And that night, God's son, Jesus, was born in a small stable. Mary wrapped him up warmly and laid him in a manger full of warm, soft hay.

On a hillside just outside Bethlehem, some shepherds were looking after their flocks of sheep. It had been a quiet, calm night and most of the shepherds had dozed off. Suddenly, the calm was shattered and sky filled with angels, brighter than the brightest stars. The shepherds were wide awake by now … and terrified.

'Don't be frightened,' the angels said. 'We bring you wonderful news. Tonight, the son of God and the saviour of the world has been born in a stable in Bethlehem. Go there now and see him.'

The shepherds set off at once, taking with them a tiny, bleating lamb to give to Jesus. When they reached the stable, they fell on their knees and praised God. And when they left, they spread the joyful news of Jesus's birth to everyone they met.

Far away in the East, three wise men, dressed in fine robes of silk and gold, were riding on their camels. A few nights earlier, they had seen a great star blazing in the sky – a sign that somewhere a new king had been born. When they reached the

city of Jerusalem, they stopped at the royal palace where they were sure they would find this new king. But the only king they found was King Herod, who was greatly alarmed at their news.

'This cannot be!' he said, furiously. 'I'm the only rightful king around here.'

Herod called his priests and asked them where this Jesus was to be born.

'Bethlehem, Your Majesty,' they replied. 'As the prophets foretold.'

Herod told the wise men what his priests had said. But in his mind was a cunning plan to find the baby himself and to get rid of him.

'When you find the baby,' he said, 'let me know so that I, too, can go and worship him.'

The wise men set off on their camels once again, and followed the star to Bethlehem. There they found Mary, Joseph and the baby Jesus. They knelt down and worshipped him and presented him with gifts of precious gold, sweet-smelling frankincense and soothing myrrh. That night, in a dream, an angel told them of Herod's plan and warned them not to return to Jerusalem. So the three wise men went home by a different route. An angel appeared to Joseph, too.

'King Herod is looking for Jesus,' the angel said, 'and wants to kill him. Take him to Egypt and stay there until it is safe to return.'

So, Mary, Joseph and Jesus left Bethlehem and set off for Egypt and safety.

HOW DAYAMANTI CHOSE HER HUSBAND

There was once an Indian princess, called Dayamanti, who was so beautiful that even the gods wanted to marry her. In fact, she had so many suitors that her father, King Bhima, decided to hold a ceremony at which his daughter would choose a husband. The four gods of the Earth, Indra, Varuna, Agni and Yama decided to attend the ceremony. They leapt into their golden chariots and sped off through the sky.

On the way, they saw a figure on the road far below them. He was so handsome and noble that he looked more like a god than a mere mortal. It was King Nala, on his way to see Dayamanti.

'Tell Dayamanti,' the gods said to the startled king, 'that she must choose one of us for her husband.'

King Nala was in despair. 'Oh, my lords, do not make me your messenger. For I wish to marry Dayamanti myself.' But the gods would not listen.

When King Nala reached Dayamanti, it was love at first sight. She was even more beautiful than he had imagined. Dayamanti, for her part, had never seen such a handsome man. But when King Nala gave her the message, her eyes filled with tears. She could not disobey the gods. What should she do?

'Tell the gods to come to the ceremony,' she said. 'You must come, too. I will choose you, fair and square. Then the gods cannot object.'

So the great day arrived. Kings and princes from far and wide arrived to woo Dayamanti, but in vain. Dayamanti only had eyes for King Nala. But which King Nala? For there before her stood five King Nalas, all dressed the same and all as handsome as each other. The gods had played a trick on her.

'My lords,' she pleaded, 'I vowed long ago to marry Nala. Please do not make me break my vow.'

'We'll give you some clues,' said the King Nalas, in unison. 'Look carefully and you will see which one of us is real.'

So Dayamanti looked as carefully as she could. Only one of the Nalas ever blinked; the others simply stared at her. Only one of the Nalas was sweating in the hot sun; the others were as cool as could be. Only one of the Nalas cast a shadow; the others cast none. And only one of the Nalas had his feet on the ground; the others were floating just above it. No doubts remained – only one of the Nalas was the true one, the one Dayamanti chose to be her husband.

THE BLUE GOD'S BIRTH

To save mankind, the Hindu god, Vishnu, has appeared on Earth nine times in nine different disguises, including a fish, a tortoise and a lion. Twice, he has appeared in human form, as the hero Rama, and as the blue god Krishna – one of the best loved gods in India. This is the story of Krishna's birth.

Long ago, the kingdom of Mathura, on the banks of the River Yamuna, was ruled by a wicked king, King Hamsa. He had thrown his father, the rightful king, into a dungeon and seized the throne for himself. Now, King Hamsa had a sister who was as sweet and kind as he was rotten and wicked. She married a handsome man, called Vasudeva, who came to live at the court.

One day, a wise man appeared at King Hamsa's court and asked for an audience with the king. 'I have important news,' he said, 'concerning the future of the kingdom.'

'Well, what is it?' boomed King Hamsa. 'I haven't got all day.'

'Your Majesty, it's about your sister, Devaki,' the wise man replied. 'Beware of her children, for her eighth child will kill you.'

The king was furious. He ranted and raged in a terrible temper.

But he was also quite frightened. So he threw his sister and her husband into prison. Now he could kill their children the moment they were born.

The years went by and Devaki had seven daughters. And King Hamsa killed them all, one after the other. Meanwhile, in their mountaintop home, the gods heard of King Hamsa's wickedness and decided to punish him.

'When Devaki's eighth child is born, Hamsa will have more than he bargained for,' Vishnu announced. 'For it will be me, born as the baby Krishna. And I shall destroy the king, once and for all.'

And so it came to be. On the eighth day of the waning Moon of August, Devaki gave birth to her eighth child, a baby boy.

'He's so beautiful,' said Devaki, with tears in her eyes. 'How I wish we could save his life.'

'You can,' said a voice, though no-one was there. 'Undo your chains, Vasudeva, and take the baby across the river to the cowherd, Nanda. Don't worry. The guards are asleep and no-one will see you go.'

Vasudeva did as he was told. For he was sure that the voice was that of the gods (and he was right). He picked up the baby and crept out of the prison. When he reached the river, his heart sank. It had been raining for days, and the river was now a raging torrent. How was he going to get across? Surely he would drown?

'Have no fear,' said the voice in his ear.

So, Vasudeva held Krishna above his head and began to wade across the river. To his alarm, the water seemed to rise higher with every step he took. Soon it had reached his shoulders. Then Krishna stretched out a tiny foot and dipped it into the river. Immediately, the waters became calm and began to go down again. Vasudeva could now continue his journey.

When he reached the other side of the river, Vasudeva went straight to the house of the cowherd, Nanda, and his wife, Yashoda. Then he returned to his prison cell to tell Devaki that their baby was safe. The following morning, King Hamsa's fury knew no bounds.

'No-one dares to trick me,' the king ranted. 'I'll find the child, and then I'll kill him.' He sent his soldiers to all four corners of the kingdom, to kill every baby boy they could find. But they didn't find Krishna. The cowherd's house was outside Hamsa's kingdom, and the soldiers were not allowed to search there.

Nanda and Yashoda loved and cared for the baby and brought him up as their own. Krishna grew up to be an extremely mischievous child, and his foster-parents never knew a dull moment. But everyone loved him and he was always able to get himself out of trouble, one way or another. So they didn't worry – they knew he could look after himself.

Many years later, another wise man visited King Hamsa's court and requested an audience with the king.

'I have come with news of Devaki's son,' he said.

'What son? What son?' roared the king. 'There's no son. He's dead, along with all the others.'

'Oh no, he isn't, Your Majesty,' the wise man replied, rather regretting he had come. And he told the king all about Krishna, his foster-parents and his exploits. 'They say he is a god,' the wise man ended, perhaps unwisely.

Needless to say, King Hamsa was beside himself with rage. And his fear returned as he remembered the prophecy. He decided to organize a wrestling competition at the palace.

'I'll pit this Krishna against the giants, Mustik and Chaur,' plotted the king, cheering up a little. 'That'll teach him. And just for good measure, I'll let loose a wild elephant too.'

But the king's wicked plan backfired, as wicked plans are liable to do. On the day of the competition, Krishna killed first the elephant, then the two giants, Mustik and Chaur, and finally he killed King Hamsa, just as the prophecy had foretold.

HOW GANESH GOT HIS ELEPHANT HEAD

The blue-throated god, Shiva, was married to a good and beautiful goddess called Parvati. Their home was high up on Mount Kailasha in the snow-capped Himalayas and they were very happy together … usually. Shiva was the creator and destroyer of the universe, a very busy god indeed, and he was often away from Mount Kailasha for years at a time. Parvati sat patiently at home, waiting for him to return. She had plenty of time to think while Shiva was away, and one thing made Parvati very sad. She desperately wanted a child, but every time she tried to talk to Shiva about it he just got crosser and crosser. She was lonely, stuck on her mountaintop all by herself, and she was bored. Then she had a wonderful idea.

'I'll show him,' she thought, smiling to herself. 'I'll make myself a baby. After all, what's the point of being a goddess if you can't do the things you want?'

So, she collected some earth from the mountainside and mixed it with water to make a soft clay. Then she began, very carefully, to mould the clay into shapes. She made a head, arms, legs, and a body with a chubby, round tummy. Soon her baby was almost complete. She picked out the features on its face and stood back to admire her work. On the ground in front of her lay a perfectly formed baby boy. Parvati was beside herself with joy. At last, she had the child she wanted. There was just one thing left to do – to bring the clay baby to life. She held it in her arms and rocked it to and fro. As she rocked, she sang:

'Now is the time for your life to begin,
Come alive, my son.'

All of a sudden, the baby opened its shining black eyes and smiled the brightest smile she had ever seen. From that moment on, Parvati and her son were never apart.

Several years passed, and still Shiva hadn't come back to Mount Kailasha. But Parvati didn't mind so much anymore. Now she had her son she didn't get lonely or bored. And she didn't feel frightened of being on her own. Her son was the best bodyguard she had ever had.

Then, one day, Shiva returned to the mountain. He was glad to be home and longing to see Parvati. But he found his way into the palace blocked by a strange, determined boy he had never seen before. Shiva was astonished. Whatever was going on? He tried to push past but the boy stood firm. Then Shiva began to get angry. He was used to having his own way, especially in his own palace, and especially when he had been away from home for so long.

'For the last time, get out of my way,' he stormed at the stubborn boy, 'or you will be very, very sorry.'

Still the boy didn't move, not a single muscle. Shiva had just about had enough. In a terrible temper, he drew out a sword and cut the boy's head off. That would teach him! Hearing the commotion, Parvati rushed out of her room. She looked at her husband – and then at her son. She screamed with horror, and began to cry. She sobbed and sobbed, as Shiva watched helplessly and in great confusion. Whatever was the matter?

'You dreadful man!' Parvati cried. 'You have murdered our son. Why did you do it? He was only a child.'

Now Shiva was even more confused. As far as he knew, they didn't have a son. But he had an uneasy feeling about all of this, and he was beginning to regret losing his temper. Then Parvati explained.

'How do you think I feel, being left here on my own all this time? There's nothing to do and no-one to talk to,' she sobbed. 'And you always get so cross when I try to talk about having a baby. So I made myself one. And now you've killed him.'

Shiva was horrified. He hadn't meant to make her so unhappy. 'I'll do anything you want,' he said to his wife. 'Anything.'

'Then bring my son back to life,' Parvati cried, and ran from the room.

Shiva sent messengers to all four corners of the universe. He told them to bring back the head of the first living creature they saw on their travels. Before long one of the messengers returned, carrying the head of a mighty elephant. Shiva fitted the elephant's head on to the boy's body, then he breathed gently on the boy, once, then twice, and brought him back to life. Parvati was delighted when she saw him. She forgave Shiva in a trice.

'Now he'll be wise like an elephant,' she said, 'as well as being beautiful and kind.'

Shiva and Parvati named their son Ganesh. And that is the story of how Ganesh got his elephant head.

THE GOLEM OF PRAGUE

Some time in the Middle Ages, in the city of Prague, the leader of the Jews was a very holy man called Rabbi Judah Lev. For many years he had lived happily in the city, preaching in the synagogue and studying his holy books. But there were many people in Prague who disliked the Jews and wanted to drive them out. One day, a child went missing from its home. The people immediately blamed the Jews.

'They have kidnapped and killed that poor child,' some cried.

'And used its blood in their wicked sacrifices,' others joined in.

Gradually the rumour spread and soon, whenever anyone went missing, it was the Jews who got the blame. It was Rabbi Judah's job to go to the court where the Jews stood trial and persuade the judge of their innocence. In no time at all he was having to attend the court almost every day.

One night, before he got into bed, Rabbi Judah prayed to God with these words:

'Dear Lord, please help me to put an end to all these lies. They are getting worse by the day. Tell me what I should do.'

He put a blank piece of paper under his pillow and went to sleep. In the morning he lifted his pillow and took out the paper. On it was written:

'To stop the lies you must make a man. He will do whatever you tell him. But, a word of warning! Destroy this man once he has carried out your bidding. Don't be tempted to use him as your servant.'

Rabbi Judah knew that these were God's words. The next day, under cover of darkness, he set out for the muddy marsh on the edge of the city. There, in the mud, he drew the outline of a giant man. He traced the letters of God's name on his forehead and said a special prayer to bring him to life. Rabbi Judah called the giant, Yossel the Golem.

On the outskirts of the city there stood an ancient castle. In it lived a Baron who had once been rich, but who had spent all of his money on gambling and drink. The Baron had a little stepdaughter, called Maria. She was rich in her own right, and the Baron often plotted how to get his hands on her money. One day, while Maria was fetching firewood from the cellar he locked her in and bolted the door. Then he went to the police and reported her missing.

'I know who's taken her,' he sobbed, 'it's those evil Jews. They have probably killed her by now.'

So the police arrested a group of Jews and put them on trial. Of course, the Jews had done nothing wrong and pleaded their innocence. But the judge found them guilty, nevertheless, and sentenced them to death. Then, all of a sudden, the courtroom door opened and in came Yossel the Golem with Maria in his arms.

'Why did you lock me in the cellar, stepfather?' Maria asked. 'I had to wait for this kind giant to let me out.'

The Baron had no choice but to own up to his part in the crime. And the Jews were set free at once, much to their and Rabbi Judah's relief.

'Now I must destroy the Golem,' Rabbi Judah resolved when he was back home again. He went over to the sleeping Golem. 'On the other hand,' thought the Rabbi, 'perhaps I could just get him to do a couple of chores first. Then I'll destroy him.' How quickly he had forgotten God's warning!

When the Golem woke up, Rabbi Judah called to him, 'Yossel, I have a little job for you. Fetch some water from the well and fill up the tank in the kitchen.'

Then the Rabbi went into his study to read his holy books. He was so engrossed in his reading he didn't notice how much time had passed. When he went back to the kitchen, it was swimming in water. The Golem hadn't known when to stop.

'I really must destroy him,' said the Rabbi. 'I'll do it tomorrow.'

But he didn't. And the longer he left it, the more the Golem led a life of his own. He went out and wandered around the city. People were afraid of him, he was so big, strong and ugly. They begged the Rabbi to destroy him.

'It's not that easy, I'm afraid,' said the Rabbi, sadly. 'He's so tall that I can't reach his forehead to rub out the name of God that is written there. I should have done it when he was asleep, but he doesn't seem to sleep much anymore.'

Rabbi Judah was almost at his wits' end. Then he had an idea. Yossel the Golem liked his food. And he liked his drink too. The Rabbi asked for a volunteer.

'I'll do it,' said a brave young girl called Miriam. She invited the Golem to her house for a drink. The Golem drank one glass of wine, then a second, then a third. He drank one bottle, then another, and then went down into the cellar and drank everything in sight. When Miriam went to find him he stood up, smiled, swayed and fell over in a deep sleep. Miriam quickly rubbed God's name from his forehead. Then the Golem shrank and shrank until all that was left of him was a small lump of mud.

Rabbi Judah was very grateful to Miriam.

'In future, oh Lord,' he prayed that night, 'I shall do exactly as you say. I have learned my lesson, once and for all!'

THE PRINCE AND THE GURU'S CLOAK

The sixth leader of the Sikhs, Guru Har Govind, became friendly with the Mughal Emperor of India, Jehangir. The Guru accompanied the emperor on hunting trips and debated religion with him, although the emperor was a Muslim and did not look kindly on other faiths. Inevitably, there were people at the Mughal court who viewed their friendship with great suspicion and even jealousy. Among these was an important official, Chandu. This is the story of how Chandu tricked Jehangir into getting rid of Guru Har Govind.

Emperor Jehangir was very ill. He lay on his bed, getting weaker by the day. He had tried cure after cure, but nothing seemed to help. Eventually, he said to Chandu, 'Chandu, summon the court astrologer. Perhaps he can foresee the future and tell me what will make me better.'

Chandu did as he was commanded. But before he allowed the court astrologer in to see the emperor, Chandu took him aside.

'If you do exactly as I say,' Chandu said to the astrologer, 'I will reward you with jewels and riches beyond your wildest dreams. Now, this is my plan ...'

The astrologer agreed to do what Chandu asked, for he was a greedy man.

Chandu took the astrologer into the darkened room where the emperor lay on his sickbed.

'Tell me, noble astrologer,' said the emperor, 'what must I do to be cured of this illness? I would do anything to feel well again.'

'Your Royal Majesty,' the astrologer said, exactly as Chandu had told him to, 'you must send a holy man to the fortress of Gwalior to pray for your health and speedy recovery.'

'Very well,' replied Jehangir. 'But who shall we send? Who is the holiest man in the empire?'

Chandu pretended to give the matter some thought. Then he said, 'What about Guru Har Govind? Surely there is no-one else as god-fearing as he?'

The emperor agreed at once and thanked his trusty friend, Chandu, for his

advice. He dispatched Guru Har Govind immediately to the fortress at Gwalior, in north-west India. The Guru did not complain about being sent away, but he could not help thinking that there was more to this than met the eye.

When Guru Har Govind reached Gwalior, he discovered that he was not alone in the fortress. Another fifty-two Hindu rajahs, or princes, were being held prisoner with him at the emperor's command. The rajahs were dirty, downhearted and constantly hungry. The Guru felt sorry for their plight and tried to help them in any way he could. Like the rajahs, he was allowed very few possessions. But what he had he shared, and his good humour helped to cheer everyone up when things looked bleak.

Weeks, then months, then one year, then two passed. Eventually news came that the emperor had at long last recovered from his illness. He had also uncovered Chandu's evil plot and wanted the Guru to return to court. But Guru Har Govind would not abandon his new-found friends. He sent a message to Jehangir.

'Your Majesty, I will be happy to return to court as soon as possible. But I cannot leave Gwalior unless the other prisoners are released with me.'

Jehangir read the note with dismay. He couldn't possibly release all fifty-two rajahs. So he sent this reply to the Guru.

'Dear friend, so be it. I shall free as many prisoners as can hold on to your cloak as you pass out of the fortress gateway.'

Guru Har Govind had to think quickly. The emperor had been clever – the gateway was extremely narrow and only a few of the princes would be able to pass through. Now the Guru had to be even cleverer. He ordered a special cloak to be made for him, with fifty-two tassels sewn along its hem. When the gates were opened to allow the Guru out, not ten, not twenty, but all fifty-two of the rajahs came out with him, each holding on to one of the tassels. It was a bit of a tight squeeze through the gateway – but they made it. Guru Har Govind and his splendid new cloak had saved them all.

HOW RAMA DEFEATED RAVANA

Do you remember the story of how Hanuman, the monkey-general, found the beautiful princess, Sita, wife of Rama? Sita was being held prisoner by the evil demon king, Ravana, on the island of Lanka. When Hanuman returned from Lanka, he brought Rama the good news that Sita was found. Rama was overjoyed. Now it was up to him to journey to Lanka and rescue her.

Rama gathered together a mighty army of thousands of monkeys and bears. Hanuman and Jambavan, the bear king, stood proudly at its head. Then Rama and his loyal brother, Lakshman, led them on the long march to the ocean.

'Follow me, brave friends,' Rama cried. 'Let us rescue Sita and destroy the demon king!'

'Victory to Rama!' the army cheered. 'Long live Rama!'

But when they reached the shores of the ocean, they stopped in their tracks. For how were they to get across the ocean? It was too far to swim. Then one of the monkeys stepped out of the crowd and bowed to Rama.

'Lord Rama,' he said, 'I have an idea. I often come down to the ocean and skim stones across the water. I could do so now and, if the god of the ocean is kind, he will keep them afloat so that they form a bridge to Lanka.'

'Clever monkey!' Rama said with a smile. 'We will help you.'

They worked all day and all night to build their bridge. When it was ready, they surged across, ready for battle.

Meanwhile, in his palace on Lanka, Ravana was watching and waiting. He summoned his brothers, generals and demon soldiers to a council of war to ask them what should be done. The first brother urged caution.

'Rama is a brave and mighty warrior,' he said. 'Many of us will die if we attempt to kill him. Let us return his wife to him, as he wishes, and so spare the bloodshed and the slaughter.' Silence fell on the council. Then Ravana spoke.

'Go!' he roared. 'Get out of my sight! You are no brother of mine, but a miserable, snivelling coward!'

So Ravana's brother left the court and went to offer his services to Rama instead. Ravana, still in a furious mood, dispatched his best general to kill Rama. But just as the general reached Rama's army, Hanuman picked him up and tossed him over his shoulder, far out into the ocean.

Then Ravana sent his second brother, a huge and terrible giant, to do away with Rama once and for all. The giant had been asleep for six months and his strength was renewed, so he had no thought of failure. But fail he did. For, once again, he was no match for Hanuman. While many of the monkeys and most of the bears ran away from the giant in fright, Hanuman stood his ground. He pulled a great tree out of the earth and brought it crashing down on the giant's head. Then Rama finished him off with an arrow from his magic bow.

When Ravana heard what had happened to his general and to his brother, he was angrier than he had ever been in his life.

'So,' he snarled, 'that is how it is to be. Well, two can play at that game. Just you wait and see.'

He called his son, Indrajit, and sent him to face Rama with an army of the wickedest demons he could find. All night the battle raged. The sky was filled with arrows and thunderbolts and spears. The ground was stained with blood as soldiers were wounded or killed. When morning came, hardly any of Rama's army was left unharmed. Monkeys and bears lay all around, groaning in pain, while Ravana laughed and clapped his son on the back. Worse was to come. As Hanuman surveyed the slaughter, he caught sight of Rama and Lakshman lying among the wounded soldiers.

'Lord Rama, Lord Rama,' Hanuman called, 'please do not die. Tell me what I must do to save your life.'

Rama opened his eyes, and whispered, 'You must fetch some healing herbs from a mountain in the Himalayas. Only they can save us.'

So Hanuman, son of the god of the wind, leapt, as he had once leapt before, right over the ocean and to the top of the mountain. There he found herbs growing all about him, hundreds and hundreds of them. But he had no idea which herbs were the healing variety.

'I'll just have to take the whole mountain,' he sighed.

And this is what he did. He lifted the whole mountain in one of his hands, and, with another gigantic leap, carried it back to Lanka and to Rama. The healing herbs were found and soon not only were Rama and Lakshman restored to health, but all of the soldiers who had been wounded or injured in the fray. The sounds of rejoicing were so loud that they reached Ravana, safe (or so he thought) in his palace.

The time had now come for Ravana to face the might of Rama. The demon king himself was going into battle. Ravana put on his armour of purest silver and gold, and strapped a pure gold helmet to each of his heads. Then, flanked by demons, he boarded his war chariot and raced towards Rama. The monkeys and bears, though trembling with fear at the sight of Ravana, took up their spears and prepared for battle. But Rama stopped them.

'My friends,' he said, 'you have fought on my behalf many times. But this is one battle I must fight for myself.'

Rama climbed into his own chariot and charged towards Ravana. The demon king showered arrows and spears down on Rama, but none seemed to touch him. Rama shot arrow after arrow in return, but still Ravana lived. Then a special arrow fitted itself into Rama's bow, an arrow with a tip of flame and shaft of gold, sent by Lord Indra. Rama took careful aim and fired. The arrow flew straight at Ravana and pierced his heart. Howls of agony from his ten mouths filled the air, then he was dead and the battle was won.

Amongst the joy and the cheering Hanuman appeared, leading Sita by the hand. And so Rama and Sita were reunited and returned home in triumph to be crowned king and queen. The monkeys and bears were not forgotten. The feasts and celebrations lasted for many weeks and, when they finally went back to their homes, the monkeys and bears were welcomed as heroes.

THE BATTLES OF BADR AND UHUD

In 622AD, the prophet Muhammed and his followers, the Muslims, were forced to leave the city of Mecca and flee to Medina. You can read about Muhammed's escape from Mecca on pages 77-8. He fled because many Meccans would not accept the new teachings of Islam and plotted to destroy Muhammed.

Two years after Muhammed left Mecca, he and his followers were attacked by an army of a thousand Meccans. Muhammed's Muslim forces numbered just three hundred and nineteen soldiers. Yet Allah sent a thousand angels to help him, and the Meccan army was defeated. This was the Battle of Badr, the first of two battles between the Muslims and the Meccans.

It was not long before the Meccans fought back in the second great battle, the Battle of Uhud. The Meccans gathered a mighty army of three thousand soldiers and two hundred horsemen and marched on Medina. A small group of Muslims, led by Muhammed, were defeated and returned to Medina. The victorious Meccans followed close behind, intent on capturing the city. A Muslim, called Salman, suggested a way of keeping them out.

'We should build a deep ditch around the city – that will keep them away.'

So the Muslims dug a ditch, and the plan worked. A month passed as the Meccan army sat outside the ditch and waited. They ran short of food and the weather began to get worse. One night, in despair, they decided to take their chance and attack the city. As they were about to strike, a terrible storm blew up. The next morning, the relieved Muslims discovered the Meccan camp in complete disarray.

Their tents had blown down and most of the soldiers had fled. Medina was safe again.

THE TEN PLAGUES OF EGYPT

The Israelite people lived in exile in Egypt for many years. For most of the time, their lives were pretty miserable. They had to work very hard, and they were often treated cruelly by their Egyptian masters. Then, one day, God spoke to Moses and said, 'You must lead your people out of Egypt and into the promised land where they can live in safety and peace. Go to the Pharaoh and tell him to let the Israelites leave Egypt. Tell him this is God's command.'

So Moses went to the Pharaoh and told him what God had said.

'Hah!' the Pharaoh replied, with a sneer. 'So what! This God of yours is no God of mine. Why should I do what he says?'

And, instead of letting the Israelites go, he made them work twice as hard and made their lives twice as miserable as they had been before. The Israelites blamed Moses for raising their hopes, only for them to be cruelly dashed. So, God decided to show the Pharaoh just how powerful he really was, and to force him to listen to his commands.

'I will send ten plagues on the land of Egypt,' God told Moses. 'Then surely the Pharaoh will listen.'

First, God turned the water of the River Nile to blood. All the fish died, and the river stank so badly that the Egyptians could not drink its water and went thirsty. Still the Pharaoh would not listen.

Then God sent a plague of frogs over Egypt. There were frogs everywhere – millions and millions of them. They hopped out of the river, out of ponds and pools. They rained down from the sky. They hopped into people's homes, into their cooking pots and water tanks. They even hopped into their beds. In despair, the Pharaoh called for Moses.

'Pray to your God,' he said, 'and ask him to get rid of these creatures. Then I will let your people go.'

So Moses prayed to God to get rid of the frogs. And he did so. But when Pharaoh saw that the frogs were gone at last, he changed his mind. He wouldn't listen to Moses' God – and he wouldn't let the Israelites go.

Then God sent a plague of flies which drove everyone mad with their buzzing and biting. The sky was black with swarms of flies. Houses were full of them. People were covered in them. Again, the Pharaoh called for Moses.

'Pray to your God,' he said, 'and ask him to get rid of these creatures. Then I will let your people go.'

So Moses prayed to God and soon the flies were gone. And again, when Pharaoh saw that they had disappeared, he changed his mind.

Then God sent a plague on the cattle, camels, horses and sheep and they died of a terrible disease. But only the animals belonging to the Egyptians died; the Israelites' animals were spared. The next plague affected the people themselves. They were covered in boils, of the reddest, sorest, most painful kind. Still, the Pharaoh would not listen. Then came hailstones that beat down on the ground, and fire that licked at the trees and made it unsafe even to set foot outside. People cowered in their homes, hoping for the storm to die down. They had never seen anything like it. And, although the Pharaoh once again begged Moses to pray for the storm to stop, again he broke his promise almost as soon as he had made it.

Things went from bad to worse. A terrible wind blew across Egypt. It lasted a day and a night, and the next morning a dreadful sight greeted the people. The whole country was covered in locusts. The locusts ate every plant and every leaf that the hail and fire had spared until there was not a single green thing left in Egypt. The plague lasted until God took pity on the Egyptians and sent another wind which blew the locusts into the sea. No sooner had the locusts gone than Egypt was covered in deep darkness which lasted for three long days. No-one moved; they didn't dare. And still the Pharaoh kept the Israelites in Egypt and hard at work.

Then God sent a tenth and final plague, the most terrible of all. One night, at midnight, the sound of weeping and wailing could be heard coming from the houses of the Egyptians. For God had sent a plague on the eldest son of every family, and they all died. Then, finally, the Pharaoh called for Moses.

'Go at once, and take your people with you,' he said. 'This time, I mean what I say. Or we shall all be dead.'

And this time, the Pharaoh kept his word. The Israelites gathered up their flocks of sheep, their cattle and belongings, and Moses led them out of Egypt towards the promised land.

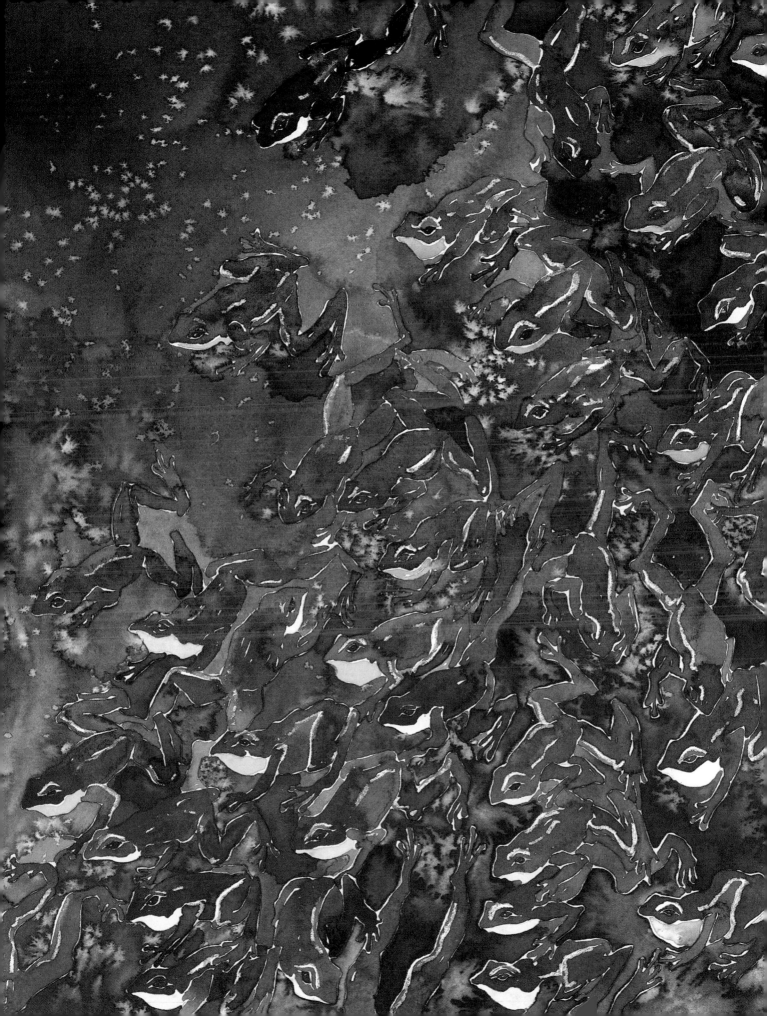

THE LIFE OF THE BUDDHA

The founder of the Buddhist faith is known as the Buddha. But this was a name given to him later in his life when, after a long time spent in meditation, he gained enlightenment and saw the truth in all things. The word 'Buddha' means 'enlightened one'. This is the story of the Buddha's life.

The Buddha was born in about 560BC in the village of Lumbini on the border of India and Nepal. His father, King Sudhodana, was the ruler of a small kingdom around Lumbini, and his mother was Queen Maya who was beautiful and pure. One night, Queen Maya dreamt that a great white elephant holding a lotus blossom in its trunk visited her while she slept. Ten months later, on the night of the full moon of May, the Buddha was born from his mother's side, in a grove of trees. He was given the name Siddhartha Gautama. The gods and all the world rejoiced. For they knew that this was no ordinary prince.

Soon after his son's birth, King Sudhodana went to consult the fortune-tellers.

'Tell me,' he said, 'what the future holds in store for my son.'

'Your Majesty,' they replied, 'if Siddhartha Gautama remains in this world, he will become the greatest ruler there has ever been – emperor of all India. But,' they continued, 'if he chooses to leave the world for a holy life, he will become a preacher without equal.'

The king wanted his son to become a great emperor, not a monk, and he did his best to make sure that this was what would happen. The young Siddhartha led a life of luxury in his father's palace, sheltered from the outside world. He had fine clothes, fine food, fine horses to ride – everything his heart could desire. When he was older Siddhartha married the beautiful Princess Yashodara. They had a son, Rahula, and life should have been full of joy. But Siddhartha was restless.

'Surely, there must be more to life than all this finery,' he thought. 'I must leave the palace and see for myself.'

The fortune-tellers had told King Sudhodana not to let his son see anyone old, sick, or dead. This is why Siddhartha was kept so well-protected inside the palace. But, one day, Siddhartha set out in his chariot for a ride. For the first time in his life he saw unhappiness and suffering. First, he saw a frail old man hobbling along the

road. Then he saw a sick man whose body was so racked with pain he could hardly walk. And then he saw a funeral procession, with a family crowded weeping around a dead relative. An old man, a sick man and a dead man. Siddhartha asked his charioteer what all this meant. The reply was simple.

'This is just what happens to all of us, at some time or another,' he was told. 'We all grow old, get sick sometimes and die in the end. That's life.'

On his next journey, Siddhartha met a monk with shaven head and yellow robes, carrying a begging bowl. The monk looked serene and free from care.

'I will follow the monk's example,' Siddhartha decided, 'and seek the truth. I must find out how people can overcome the sufferings of life.'

So, one night, under cover of darkness, Prince Siddhartha Gautama left his father's palace, his wife and son, and all his worldly goods behind and set off into the world. For seven years he wandered in search of truth and knowledge. Two famous teachers taught him yoga to exercise his mind and body, but this did not help him. Then some holy men told him that only a strict life of prayer and fasting would lead him to the truth. But this only made him ill. So, Siddhartha left the holy men and set off on his way again. When he came to a place called Bodh Gaya, he sat down under the spreading branches of a fig tree to meditate.

For forty-nine days and forty-nine nights, Siddhartha meditated. When he opened his eyes he knew he had found the truth he had been seeking. He was now the Buddha, the enlightened one. Now he knew that people suffered because they were never content with what they had. They always wanted something more. They were never satisfied and never at peace with themselves.

'I must teach people new ways of acting and thinking,' he vowed, 'so they do not want what they haven't got, and do not suffer for wanting it.'

And this is what the Buddha did. For the next forty-five years, until he died at the age of eighty, the Buddha wandered all over India, living as a monk and preaching his message. Soon he was joined by a band of loyal monks and nuns, including his own son, Rahula, who walked with him and helped to spread his wise words.

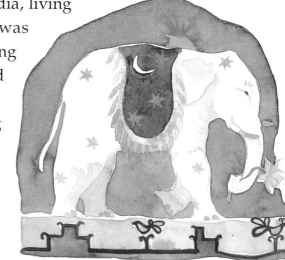

Just before the Buddha died, he told his grieving followers and friends:

'Hold fast to the truth, as you would to a lamp,
And strive to become free from evil.'

MUHAMMED ESCAPES FROM MECCA

This story tells of the escape of the Prophet Muhammed, the founder of Islam, from Mecca to Medina, in Saudi Arabia. These two cities are the most important places of pilgrimage for Muslims today. Muhammed's journey is called the hijra, or 'flight'. It happened in 622AD, the year that marks the start of the Islamic calendar.

The Prophet Muhammed was born and lived for many years in the city of Mecca. It was here that he heard the word of Allah, and here that he began to teach people about Islam. Many Meccans listened eagerly to what he had to say but there were some who did not want to hear. The rich merchants of the city were afraid of losing their power and prestige if people started to believe in Muhammed's god, and they plotted how best to get rid of him. Soon neither Muhammed nor any of his followers were safe as long as they remained in Mecca.

One night, a group of the richest and most powerful merchants met in secret, to plan what to do.

'We must kill him,' one said.

'Easier said than done,' said another. 'He's got some powerful friends.'

'I wouldn't like to be the one to do it,' another agreed. 'Whoever kills him won't live long himself.'

There were murmurs of agreement from all around. But what were they to do? Then a merchant called Abu Jahl spoke out.

'Let each of us send a man to wait outside the Prophet's house. When he comes out to pray in the morning, they will all help to kill him. Then one person cannot be blamed.'

'A very good plan,' the other merchants agreed. 'His friends couldn't possibly take revenge on us all!'

But Muhammed had been warned. The Angel Jibril told him in a dream that he would not be safe sleeping in his house that night. So the Prophet asked his cousin,

Ali, to take his place, assuring him that he would come to no harm.

As night fell, the merchants' men gathered outside Muhammed's house. They waited, silent and deadly, until dawn. Then the door opened, and they all sprang forward, knives in hand. But the man who came out was not the Prophet. Furious at being tricked, the men reported back to the merchants.

All this gave Muhammed a chance to make his escape. His friend, Abu Bakr, was standing by with two swift camels to carry them over the desert to the city of Medina, and to safety. But their enemies were sure to follow, so to keep them guessing Muhammed and Abu Bakr set off in the opposite direction. They travelled as fast and as far as they could that night, then they found a cool, shady cave in which to hide and shelter from the burning desert sun. Hot on their heels came the merchants and their men.

'What shall we do?' asked Abu Bakr, anxiously. 'They're sure to find us here – they'll see the entrance. Then we'll be done for.'

'Have no fear, my friend,' Muhammed reassured him. 'Allah will protect us.'

Minutes later, they heard voices outside the cave. The merchants had found the entrance, as Abu Bakr had feared.

'Look, a cave,' one voice said, 'they must be hiding in there.'

'Don't be silly,' another voice replied. 'It's just an old cave. No-one's been near it for years. Look at that spider's web right across the entrance, and that dove sitting on its nest. Nothing has disturbed them, that's for sure.'

'Oh, you're probably right,' said the first voice. 'Let's go then. They must be somewhere else.'

When Abu Bakr heard the men move away, he breathed a sigh of relief. But he was also puzzled.

'There weren't any spiders or doves when we came in here,' he said. 'How did they get there?'

Muhammed smiled. Allah had protected them, as Muhammed knew he would.

They stayed in the cave for a few days more, until they felt that the danger was well and truly passed. Then they continued their journey across the desert to a warm welcome in Medina, the city of the Prophet.

ABRAHAM
AND THE IDOLS

Abraham was one of the founding fathers of the Jewish and Christian religions. God told Abraham that he would be the ancestor of a great people who would live in the promised land of Israel. This is one of the many stories about Abraham's life.

Abraham and his family lived in the city of Haran, in the country which today we call Turkey. His father, Terah, was a craftsman. He had a little shop where he sold the fine clay statues he made. People came from far and wide to buy Terah's statues. Then they took them home, set them up on altars and worshipped these idols with prayers and offerings of sweets and flowers. Abraham couldn't understand it.

'Why are they worshipping lumps of clay?' he asked his father. 'They don't really believe they are gods, do they?'

But Terah just gave his son a clip round the ear and told him to get back to work and not waste his time with stupid questions.

Abraham helped his father in the shop. His job was to sell the statues his father made. He wasn't much good at it. One day, an old man came into the shop and pointed to a statue he wanted to buy. But before he could speak, Abraham had asked him a question.

'How old are you?' he said to the man.

'Sixty-five,' replied the man, rather taken aback, 'if it's any of your business!'

'Sixty-five?' Abraham said. 'And you're putting your faith in a statue that's not yet a day old?'

The man didn't reply. He hadn't come here to be insulted so he turned round and left, without buying anything at all.

Then an old woman came through the door, weeping and wringing her hands. Her house had been burgled and her idols stolen.

'I'll show them,' she wailed. 'I'm going to buy the biggest idol you've got, to protect me!'

But Abraham was having none of it.

'Why will that be any better?' he said to the startled woman. 'How can any idols protect you, if they can't protect themselves?'

Needless to say, the woman didn't stop to hear any more. When word reached Abraham's father about what had happened, he was furious.

'You great good for nothing!' he cried. 'There are people queuing up to buy my statues, and you haven't sold a single one. You're costing me a fortune!'

That night, Abraham kept thinking about the statues and wondering how people could think they were gods. His thoughts kept him awake so he got up and went outside. Hundreds of stars twinkled in the inky blackness of the sky.

'How beautiful the stars are,' Abraham thought. 'Surely they must be gods, if anything is.' And he began to worship them.

Then the Moon appeared, round and full.

'But the Moon is bigger and even more beautiful,' thought Abraham, interrupting his prayers. 'It must be an even more powerful god.' So he began to worship the Moon. And there he stayed, all night until daybreak. Then the Moon faded from sight and the Sun, bright and red, began to rise.

Abraham began to worship the Sun; then the cloud that blocked out the Sun's light; then the wind that blew the cloud away. Each time he started to pray, something bigger or more powerful appeared and became the object of his worship. Then, all of a sudden, the wind dropped.

'Where can it have gone?' thought Abraham. 'I didn't see anything blow it away.' Then he realized that behind the wind, the stars, the Moon and the Sun, there must lie a greater force, a more powerful God that could not be seen or felt.

'This is the God I will worship,' Abraham decided.

He crept back into the shop, taking care not to wake his father. Then he picked up a large, heavy hammer and smashed every idol in sight, apart from the biggest one. He stood this idol in the middle of the shop and laid the hammer next to it.

Terah couldn't believe his eyes when he woke up and saw his devastated shop.

'What on Earth has happened?' he asked Abraham. 'Who can have done this?'

'It must have been the idols,' Abraham replied. 'Look, the big one is standing there so smugly with its hammer by its side – it must have smashed the others to bits. They were probably quarrelling. Why don't you ask it if you don't believe me?'

'What did you say?' roared his father. 'Idols can't quarrel! They can't even speak, you stupid boy!'

'Well,' said Abraham, 'if they can't even speak, how can people worship them. How can they be gods?'

His father was silent. He didn't know. Then Abraham told him about his discovery, that behind everything there was a greater God, powerful and invisible. And Terah began to worship him too.

THE LIFE OF GURU NANAK

These episodes are from a collection of stories called the Janam Sakhis, about the life of Guru Nanak (1469-1539), the founder and the first Guru of the Sikh religion.

Guru Nanak loved to travel. His faithful companion on many of his journeys was a musician called Mardana. On this occasion, Guru Nanak and Mardana had reached the city of Multan after a long, hot and tiring journey. Mardana was looking forward to a good meal and a long rest, for they been on the road for almost a week. So, anticipating the comforts ahead, Mardana followed his master through the city gates.

In Guru Nanak's time, the ancient city of Multan was famous far and wide for its priests and holy men. People came from miles around to seek their advice about all manner of things. In return for advice, the people thanked the priests with gifts of money, silk or jewellery. In no time at all, the priests and holy men of Multan grew rich and greedy. When they heard that Guru Nanak was to visit their city, they were not best pleased.

'We don't want him here,' one priest said. 'He'll be bad for business.'

'I agree,' said another, 'but what can we do to stop him?'

They put their heads together and came up with a plan. It went like this. When Guru Nanak arrived, they would send a messenger to him with a bowl of milk. The bowl would be filled to the brim, so full that not a single drop more would fit in. The message for the Guru would be this:

'There are enough holy men and priests in this city already. And there's no room for any more – not a single one.'

The messenger carried the bowl, slowly and carefully, to Guru Nanak. His eyes never left the milk, in case a drop should be spilt. He held the bowl out towards the Guru.

'My masters have sent you this bowl of milk, your holiness,' he said. 'Do you have any message for them in return?'

Mardana looked at the bowl of milk. It looked so cool and tempting, and he was so thirsty. He longed for the Guru to take the bowl so they could have a drink. But the Guru didn't. Instead, he stooped down and picked a delicate jasmine flower from a nearby bush, and dropped it into the bowl of milk. The flower filled the bowl of milk with its sweet smell. It was so fragile and light that not a single drop of milk was spilt.

Then the Guru told the messenger, 'This is my message for your masters. Just as there is room in this bowl of milk for a jasmine flower to fill it with scent, so there is always room in the world for more goodness and holiness.'

Mardana smiled at the Guru's wise words. Going thirsty was a small price to pay. And when the priests and holy men received the Guru's message, they were truly ashamed of their selfish behaviour. They went straight to Guru Nanak to say they were sorry, and to welcome him and Mardana into Multan.

This is another story from the Janam Sakhis, the stories of Guru Nanak's life. One of Guru Nanak's most important teachings was that people should live honest and selfless lives, helping those in need whenever they could.

On another of his journeys, Guru Nanak travelled to the great city of Lahore. In that city there lived a very rich banker, called Duni Chand. He had more money than most people could ever dream of, and he lived in the grandest of palaces, surrounded by gold and silver and precious objects of all kinds.

When Duni Chand heard of Guru Nanak's arrival, he rushed out to meet him.

'It would give me untold pleasure, your holiness,' he wheedled, 'if you would accept my invitation to a special feast in your honour.'

The Guru accepted the invitation and Duni Chand rushed home again to give orders to his cook and servants. He rather liked bossing people about.

Every one of the fifty guests agreed – the feast was a triumph. The food was sumptuous, the music was splendid and their host made sure they wanted for nothing. Duni Chand beamed with pleasure. When the feasting was over, he turned to Guru Nanak.

'Your holiness,' he began, 'I am one of the richest and most important men in Lahore. So, if there is anything I can do for you, you only have to ask.'

Guru Nanak thought for a few moments without replying. He looked around at the guests dressed in all their finery, at the golden plates and goblets, and at all the glittering luxury of the palace. Then he reached into his pocket and pulled out a small, simple, wooden box. He opened the lid. Inside there lay a fine, silver needle. Guru Nanak picked up the needle and handed it to Duni Chand. With a smile, he said,

'Yes, there is something you can do, my friend. You can look after this needle for me. Keep it safe and give it back to me when we meet again in the next world.'

'With pleasure, with pleasure,' said Duni Chand in a simpering voice. 'With the greatest of pleasure!'

When Guru Nanak and the other guests had left, Duni Chand ran to his wife, full of his own importance.

'Guru Nanak must have the utmost faith in me,' he cried, 'to have entrusted me with such a task. He must think very highly of me!'

'And what is this important task, dear husband?' asked his wife.

Almost bursting with pride, Duni Chand showed her the needle and repeated what the Guru had said to him.

'I am to give it back to him when we meet again in heaven,' he said.

His wife burst into peals of laughter. She laughed and laughed until her sides ached and tears ran down her cheeks. This was not the reaction Duni Chand had had in mind.

'Whatever is the matter?' he said, rather put out.

'Oh, my poor, dear husband,' she replied, gasping for breath, 'I think you had better go and ask the Guru just how you're going to be able to take the needle to heaven with you!'

Puzzled, and not a little disappointed by his wife's words, Duni Chand set off after Guru Nanak who was just disappearing down the street.

'Guru Nanak, oh Guru Nanak,' he called, 'please tell me, how will I be able to take this needle with me when I go to heaven?'

Guru Nanak stopped and looked at Duni Chand, a smile on his lips and a twinkle in his eyes.

'But Duni Chand,' he replied, 'if you can't find a way of taking a simple needle with you, what are you going to do with all those riches and precious things you have? How are you going to be able to take them to heaven when you die? The only things you will be able to take with you are good deeds and kind words. Everything else will have to be left behind.'

Duni Chand lowered his head in shame when he realized what the Guru was telling him. All his fine things were worth nothing. He couldn't take them with him when he died. It would be far better to use his great wealth to help people in need. So that is what he did. And when he died and went to heaven, he took a great many good deeds and kind words with him.

THE MERCHANT AND THE FIVE HUNDRED GOLD COINS

A few days before he died, the eighth Sikh Guru (leader), Har Krishan, told his followers that his successor would be found in the small village of Bakala near Amritsar in north-west India. Little did he realize the chaos his words would cause! All of a sudden it seemed as if every other man in Bakala was coming forward and claiming that he, and no-one else, was the true 'Baba Bakale' and Har Krishan's rightful heir. Of course, it was money they were after, for at that

time the Sikh movement was quite prosperous. Wealthy devotees often gave large donations to the Gurus to use in their work with the poor and needy. No true Guru would ever use the money for his own ends. But there were many unscrupulous people about who wanted a share of the spoils. This is the story of how a wealthy merchant, called Makhan Shah, discovered the true identity of the next and ninth Sikh Guru.

Makhan Shah was a wealthy merchant, with a flourishing trade in fine silks and exotic perfumes. He was sailing along the west coast of India with a large cargo of goods when a storm blew up out of nowhere. Makhan Shah had never seen a storm like it in all his years of sailing. The wind howled like a mad thing and the rain lashed down in great torrents from the dark, angry sky. Thunder boomed and lightning crackled. Makhan Shah's small ship was tossed to and fro, helplessly swept along by waves as high as houses. Makhan Shah and the rest of his crew were soaking wet, chilled to the bone and scared stiff. And the storm showed no signs of abating. Despite the best efforts of his crew, Makhan Shah was sure that he and his ship would not survive much longer. In despair, he closed his eyes and began to pray.

'Dear God, please hear my prayer and save my ship from drowning. I will give the Guru five hundred gold coins in thanks if you can guide us safely ashore.'

When Makhan Shah opened his eyes, he was astonished to see that the sea was calm, the sky was blue, and, most truly amazing of all, dry land loomed directly ahead. His prayers had been answered. As he guided his ship safely into harbour, Makhan Shah had never felt so grateful and relieved in all his life.

The first thing that Makhan Shah did on reaching solid ground was to remember the promise he had made to God. He set off at once on the long journey to the village of Bakala, where he was told he would find the Guru. But as soon as he arrived in the village, Makhan Shah found himself faced with a most puzzling dilemma. There were hundreds of gurus in Bakala, all claiming to be the one true Guru he sought. Makhan Shah was flummoxed. Which one of them could he believe? More importantly, to which one should he give his five hundred gold coins? After a while, he had an idea.

'I know what I'll do,' he said to himself. 'I'll visit each of these supposed gurus in turn and offer every one of them two gold coins. The fake gurus will simply take the money, no questions asked. Only the true Guru will know exactly how much I promised to donate and wonder where the rest of the money is!'

So he set off on a grand tour of the village. In the first house he entered a man was sitting cross-legged on a jewel-encrusted throne. Makhan Shah bowed and placed two gold coins in his hand.

'You have done well, my son,' said the man. 'From among all these tricksters, you have found the one true Guru. Your gift is most welcome. And your jacket is a very fine garment, too,' he added, peering at the rich silver embroidery on Makhan Shah's jacket with a greedy glint in his eye. Makhan Shah left as quickly as he could. How many more fake gurus to go?

By the time he reached the tenth imposter, Makhan Shah had begun to despair. It was the same with each of the so-called gurus in each of the houses he visited. Every one praised him for his cleverness in finding the one true Guru, and grabbed the two gold coins with glee. But none of them knew anything about his promise or asked him about the other four hundred and ninety-eight coins he had pledged. Makhan Shah wanted to keep his promise. After all, he owed his life to God. But it wasn't proving easy.

As a last resort, he asked an old man if he knew of any other gurus living in the village. The old man thought for a while and tugged at his beard. Then he said,

'There's a man who lives at the edge of the village, over there. Called Tegh Bahadur. He's a quiet man – seems to pray a lot. He might be the person you're looking for.'

Makhan Shah thanked the old man and set off in the direction he had pointed out. At the edge of the village he found a small, simple hut and, inside, Tegh Bahadur praying quietly. Makhan Shah bowed and placed two gold coins in his hand.

Tegh Bahadur looked at Makhan Shah, then he looked at the two gold coins. Then he looked at Makhan Shah again.

'Have you forgotten your promise already?' he said, gently. 'When you were about to be drowned, the figure you mentioned was five hundred gold coins, I seem to remember, not two!'

Makhan Shah was overjoyed. At last he had found the one true Guru and could keep his promise. He gladly gave the five hundred gold coins to Tegh Bahadur, then rushed out into the village to spread the good news.

'I've found Tegh Bahadur,' he announced, joyfully, 'the one true Guru!'

And that is the story of how Makhan Shah found the ninth Guru of the Sikhs. There was great rejoicing in Bakala that night.

THE LAST SUPPER

The events leading up to Jesus's death are remembered every Easter in the Christian Church. This is what happened.

Jesus and his disciples had come to Jerusalem to celebrate the Passover festival. Jesus knew that his life was in danger, for the priests and the Romans wanted to be rid of this man whom they considered to be a dangerous influence. This special Passover feast, therefore, was to be the last supper he and his twelve closest disciples would have together.

Jesus and his disciples sat down at the long table on which the Passover lamb, bread and wine stood waiting for them. Their mood was sombre and sad.

'I am glad to have this chance to be with you,' Jesus said. 'For it will be the last time we all eat together in this life.'

Nobody spoke. The disciples didn't know what to say. Then Jesus picked up some bread, blessed it and broke it into pieces. He gave a piece of the bread to each of his disciples.

'Eat this bread,' he said, 'in memory of me. For this is my body.'

Then he picked up his goblet of wine and passed it to each of them in turn.

'Drink this wine,' he said, 'for this is my blood which I will shed so that everyone's sins will be forgiven.'

They ate their meal in silence. When they had finished, Jesus broke the silence with words that sent shivers down their spines.

'One more thing I must tell you,' he said, deeply troubled. 'One of you sitting here will betray me.'

The disciples couldn't believe their ears. They all began to talk at once, to deny this terrible accusation. But Jesus was certain.

'But who will it be, Lord?' asked Peter. 'Which one of us will betray you?'

Before Jesus could answer, there was a commotion at the end of the table. One of the twelve disciples, Judas Iscariot, rushed from the table, knocking over his chair in his haste. Jesus had no need to speak – the answer was plain to see. Judas would betray him.

Later that night, Jesus went with his disciples to the Garden of Gethsemane. While they were praying, Judas arrived with the temple soldiers, for he had made a pact with the priests to betray Jesus in return for thirty pieces of silver.

'The man I kiss is the one you want,' he whispered to the soldiers. Then he went straight up to Jesus.

'Greetings, Master,' he said, and kissed Jesus on the cheek. Immediately the soldiers grabbed Jesus and took him away. There was nothing the disciples could do. Judas fled too, ashamed of what he had done. The soldiers took Jesus to the temple, where the priests were waiting for him. Now they had captured him the priests had to find a good reason to have Jesus killed. They questioned him long into the night, hoping to catch him out. But Jesus said nothing. Finally, the high priest himself asked a question.

'Are you the son of God?' he said.

'I am,' replied Jesus.

'Blasphemy! Blasphemy!' the other priests cried.

'He claims to be God,' said another, 'when he's not – when he can't be.'

'He must die for his blasphemy,' they all agreed.

The priests took Jesus to the Roman governor, Pontius Pilate. They needed Pilate's permission to have Jesus put to death. But Pilate was in a dilemma. He didn't want to antagonize the priests, but he knew that Jesus didn't deserve to be sentenced to death. So he led Jesus outside and showed him to the crowd waiting there.

'It's my custom to free one of the prisoners at your Passover time,' he told the people. 'Which one shall it be? Shall I free Jesus?'

'No,' shouted the crowd, 'free Barabbas instead!' For the priests had bribed the people to say this. 'And let Jesus be crucified!'

Pilate had no choice but to free Barabbas and deliver Jesus over to the soldiers.

Jesus was led to Golgotha, the Place of the Skull, and there they nailed him to a cross and crucified him, with one criminal to his left and another to his right.

'Forgive them, Lord God,' Jesus prayed, 'for they do not understand what they are doing.'

All day Jesus hung on the cross, growing steadily weaker. When night fell, Jesus cried out, 'It's over now!' and with those words he died.

Some of Jesus's followers begged Pilate to let them have his body so they could bury it properly. Pilate agreed – he was still feeling guilty. Jesus's followers wrapped the body in a white robe and took it to a tomb cut out of rock. They rolled a heavy stone across the entrance to the tomb and went home, on the saddest day of their lives.

Three days passed before Mary Magdalene and some of the disciples returned to the tomb. To their amazement, the stone had been rolled away and the tomb was empty. Jesus's body was nowhere to be seen. The two disciples went to tell the others but Mary stayed by the tomb, crying quietly. Suddenly she looked up. A man was standing close by.

'Why are you crying?' he said in a kindly voice. 'What has happened?'

She began to tell him about the empty tomb and how worried they all were, when he stopped her.

'Don't you recognize me, Mary?' he said. 'It is I, Jesus. Go and tell my friends that I am alive. And don't be sad anymore.'

Overjoyed, Mary ran to tell the disciples what she had seen. At first they didn't believe her – it must be too good to be true. But reports soon reached them that other people had also seen Jesus. And then, one day, he came to see them. At first they thought he must be a ghost. But he showed them the marks of the nails in his hands and feet, and he ate the fish and honey they gave him.

Jesus told the disciples to go and tell everyone they met that he had died and risen again for them, so that everyone, no matter who they were, might be forgiven for their sins and live good and honest lives. Then he took his leave of them. While they watched, he climbed a hill and was carried by a cloud up into heaven.

RELIGIONS - FACT FILES

Most of the stories in this book come from seven of the world's greatest religions. Between them, these religions have millions of followers. In these fact files you can find out more about the religions of the world – their founders, key figures, holy books, festivals and sacred sites. Of course, there isn't room here to include everything about each religion or to include information about some of the other beliefs and faiths in the book. But you will be able to find out more about all these religions in other books – and it should make fascinating reading!

BUDDHISM

WHEN AND WHERE IT BEGAN: 6th century BC, in India.
FOUNDER FIGURE: Siddhartha Gautama (c. 563-483BC), later called the Buddha, the 'enlightened one'.
MAJOR DEITIES: there are no gods in Buddhism but one important ideal is the Bodhisattva. This is someone who is ready to reach enlightenment and Nirvana, but postpones this in order to help other people.
PLACES OF WORSHIP: temples, monasteries.
SACRED PLACES: Lumbini (the Buddha's birthplace); Bodh Gaya (where the Buddha gained enlightenment); Sarnath (where the Buddha preached his first sermon); Lhasa, Tibet (for Tibetan Buddhists).
HOLY BOOKS: Tripitaka (Pali Canon), amongst others.
MAJOR FESTIVALS: May Full Moon (celebration of the Buddha's birth, enlightenment and death).

WHERE PRACTISED: Nepal, Burma, Sri Lanka, Tibet, Japan and South-East Asia; Buddhism is also becoming very popular in Western countries.
Stories from the Buddhist religion can be found on pages 36-9, 46-7, 74-6.

CHRISTIANITY

WHEN AND WHERE IT BEGAN: 1st century AD, in Palestine (now Israel).
FOUNDER FIGURE: Jesus of Nazareth (c. 4BC-29AD), also called Jesus Christ.
MAJOR DEITIES: Christians believe in one supreme God and in Jesus as the Son of God on Earth.
PLACES OF WORSHIP: churches, cathedrals.
SACRED PLACES: sites associated with Jesus's life, for example, Bethlehem (where he was born) and Jerusalem (where he died).
HOLY BOOKS: the Bible, particularly the New Testament.
MAJOR FESTIVALS: Christmas (birth of Jesus); Easter (Jesus's death and resurrection).
WHERE PRACTISED: worldwide.
Stories from the Christian religion can be found on pages 18-20, 50-2, 71-3, 90-2.

HINDUISM

WHEN AND WHERE IT BEGAN: about 2500BC, in India.
FOUNDER FIGURE: none.
MAJOR DEITIES: Hindus worship thousands of gods and goddesses. The most important gods are those of the trinity – Brahma, the creator; Vishnu, the preserver; Shiva, the creator.
PLACES OF WORSHIP: temples and shrines at home.
SACRED PLACES: the River Ganges; seven sacred cities in India – Varanasi, Hardwar, Mathura, Ayodhya, Ujjain, Dwarka, Kanchipuram.
HOLY BOOKS: Rig Veda;Upanishads;Bhagavad Gita.
MAJOR FESTIVALS: Holi (spring festival – March/April); Ram Lila (Rama's life – September);

Diwali (festival of lights – October/ November).

WHERE PRACTISED: mainly India and Nepal but also wherever Hindus have settled.

Stories from the Hindu religion can be found on pages 11-15, 29-31, 43-5, 52-9, 66-9.

ISLAM

WHEN AND WHERE IT BEGAN: AD610, in Mecca, Saudi Arabia.

FOUNDER FIGURE: the prophet, Muhammed.

MAJOR DEITIES: Muslims believe in one God, Allah, who revealed his wishes and commandments to Muhammed.

PLACES OF WORSHIP: mosques.

SACRED PLACES: Mecca (Muhammed's birthplace); Medina, Saudi Arabia; Dome of the Rock, Jerusalem.

HOLY BOOKS: the Koran.

MAJOR FESTIVALS: Day of Hijra (New Year's Day); Ramadan (month of fasting); Id Al-Fitr (end of Ramadan); Dhu Al-Hijja (month of Haj pilgrimages to Mecca).

WHERE PRACTISED: Middle East, North Africa, India, Pakistan and Bangladesh, South-East Asia and all over the world wherever Muslims have settled.

Stories from Islam can be found on pages 40-2, 48-9, 70, 77-9.

JUDAISM

WHEN AND WHERE IT BEGAN: about 1000 BC in Palestine (now Israel).

FOUNDER FIGURES: Moses and the three patriarchs – Abraham, Isaac and Jacob.

MAJOR DEITIES: Jews believe in one God who is the creator and ruler of the world.

PLACES OF WORSHIP: synagogues.

SACRED PLACES: Wailing Wall, Jerusalem; Mount Sinai

HOLY BOOKS: Hebrew Bible; Torah (the first five books of the Bible); Talmud.

MAJOR FESTIVALS: Rosh Hashanah (New Year's Day –

September/October); Yom Kippur (Day of Atonement); Hanukkah (Festival of Lights – December); Passover (March/April).

WHERE PRACTISED: Israel and all over the world wherever Jews have settled.

Stories from the Jewish religion can be found on pages 32-4, 60-2, 71-3, 80-2.

SHINTO

When and where it began: first written down in the 5th century AD but practised long before that in Japan.

FOUNDER FIGURE: none.

MAJOR DEITIES: Amaterasu, the Sun goddess; millions of gods called kami.

PLACES OF WORSHIP: shrines.

SACRED PLACES: The most important pilgrimage shrines are on the island of Honshu, for example in Ise, Izumo, Nara and Kyoto.

HOLY BOOKS: Kojiki; Nihongi; Yengishiki.

MAJOR FESTIVALS: Many cities have festivals, for example, the Gion festival in Kyoto and the Chichibu festival in Chichibu, near Tokyo.

WHERE PRACTISED: Japan.

A story from the Shinto religion can be found on pages 16-17.

SIKHISM

WHEN AND WHERE IT BEGAN: at the end of the 15th century, in Punjab, India/Pakistan.

FOUNDER FIGURE: Guru Nanak (1469-1539).

MAJOR DEITIES: one God who is considered the ultimate and eternal Guru. Ten earthly gurus brought God's word to the people.

PLACES OF WORSHIP: Gurdwaras.

SACRED PLACES: the Golden Temple, Amritsar, India.

HOLY BOOKS: Guru Granth Sahib.

WHERE PRACTISED: India and wherever Sikhs have settled in the world.

Stories from the Sikh religion appear on pages 63-6, 82-9.

WHO'S WHO?

This Who's Who is a guide to the main gods, mortals and other characters that appear throughout this book. It can also be used as an index, by referring to the pages numbers given at the end of each entry.

ABRAHAM One of the founding fathers of the Jewish and Christian religions. Pages 80-2

ADAM In the Old Testament of the Jewish and Christian Bible, Adam was the first man on Earth. Page 20

AGNI Hindu god of fire. Pages 52-3

ALLAH The supreme and only God of the Islamic faith. Pages 40-2, 48-9, 77-8

AMATERASU Japanese sun goddess, born from Izanagi's left eye. Also worshipped as the ancestor of the Japanese royal family. Page 17

BAIAME The most important god of the Australian Aborigines. Baiame is the creator of the world. Pages 8-10

BRAHMA One of the three gods of the Hindu trinity (the three most important gods in Hinduism). Brahma is the creator. Pages 11,14

BUDDHA The title given to Siddhartha Gautama, the founder of the Buddhist religion. The word 'Buddha' means 'enlightened one' or 'awakened one'. The Buddha lived in India in the 6th century BC. Pages 36-9, 46-7, 74-6

DAYAMANTI Daughter of Bhima, king of Vidarbha, India. Pages 52-3

DEVAKI Sister of King Hamsa, and Krishna's mother. Pages 54-6

EVE In the Old Testament of the Jewish and Christian Bible, Eve was the first woman on Earth. Page 20

GABRIEL The archangel sent by God to tell Mary that she would be the mother of Jesus. See Jibril. Page 50

GANESH The elephant-headed son of Shiva and Parvati. Worshipped as a guardian spirit and god of good beginnings. Page 59

HANUMAN The Hindu monkey-god; faithful friend of Rama and leader of the monkey army sent to rescue Sita. Pages 43-5, 66-9

HAR GOVIND Sixth guru (leader) of the Sikhs. Pages 63-6

HEROD King of Jerusalem at the time of Jesus's birth. Page 52

INDRA Hindu god of war, rain and storms Pages 13, 14, 52-3

IZANAGI Japanese god who, together with his wife, Izanami, created the world. Pages 16-17

IZANAMI Japanese goddess who, together with her husband, Izanagi, created the world. Pages 16-17

JESUS The founder of Christianity who was born in about 4BC in Bethlehem. His life and teaching is told in the New Testament of the Christian Bible. Christians believe that Jesus is the son of God. Pages 50-2, 90-2

JIBRIL An archangel who revealed Allah's will to Muhammed and told Maryam of her son's birth. See Gabriel. Pages 48-9, 77-8

JOSEPH In Christianity, the earthly father of Jesus. Pages 50-2

JUDAH LEV Rabbi, and leader of the Jewish community in Prague. Pages 60-2

JUDAS ISCARIOT Disciple of Jesus who betrayed him to the temple priests in return for thirty silver pieces. Pages 90-1

KRISHNA One of the most popular Hindu gods; in fact, the god Vishnu in disguise. Pages 54-6

LAKSHMI Hindu goddess of beauty and good fortune. Wife of Vishnu, the preserver. Page 15

MAHEO The great spirit and creator of the Cheyenne North American Indians. Maheo created the world out of a ball of mud. Pages 23-4

MANU In Hindu mythology, the first man on Earth. Manu was saved from the great flood by a giant fish, which was in fact Vishnu in one of his earthly disguises. Pages 29-31

MARY In Christianity, the mother of Jesus. Pages 50-2

MARYAM In the Muslim Koran, the name given to Mary, the mother of Jesus. Pages 48-9

MAYA Queen Maya, the Buddha's mother. Page 74

MESSIAH In the Muslim Koran, the name given to Maryam's son, that is, to Jesus. Pages 48-9

MOSES Founding father of the Jewish and Christian religions. Led the people of Israel out of slavery in Egypt and into their own land. Pages 71-2

MUHAMMED The prophet and founder of Islam. Allah spoke to him through the Angel Jibril. Muhammed lived from about 570-632AD. Pages 70, 77-8

MUKULU An African spirit of good and the creator of the first people on Earth. Pages 22-3

NANAK The first guru (leader) and the founder of the Sikh religion. Guru Nanak lived from 1469-1539. Pages 82-6

NANDA Cowherd, and foster-father of Krishna. Page 56

NOAH In the Old Testament of the Bible, the man chosen by God to survive the great flood. Pages 26, 32-4

NUH The Noah of the Muslim Koran. Page 26

OLD SPIDER In Polynesian mythology, a god in the form of a huge spider who created the world inside a giant clamshell. Pages 21-2

PAN GU In Chinese mythology, a giant, a god and the son of the two creative forces, Yin and Yang. Page 24

PARVATI Hindu goddess, wife of Shiva and mother of the elephant-head god, Ganesh. Pages 57-9

PETER Also known as Simon Peter. One of Jesus's closest friends and disciples. A leader of the early Christians after Jesus's death. Page 90

PONTIUS PILATE Roman governor of Jerusalem in Jesus's time. Pages 91-2

RAHU One of the most evil demons of Hindu mythology. The name 'Rahu' means 'seizer'. Rahu is believed to cause eclipses by seizing the Sun and the Moon. Pages 13-14

RAMA A Hindu god and hero; in fact, the god, Vishnu, in disguise. Married to Sita. Pages 43-5, 54, 66-9

RAVANA The ten-headed, twenty-armed demon king of Lanka (the island of Sri Lanka). Pages 43-5, 66-9

SHIVA One of the three gods of the Hindu trinity (the three most important gods in Hinduism). Shiva is the destroyer. Parvati is his wife, and Ganesh his son. Pages 11-15, 57-9

SIDDHARTHA GAUTAMA The real name of the Buddha. Pages 74-6

SITA The wife of Rama, who joined him in exile and was kidnapped by Ravana. Pages 43-5, 66-9

SUDHODANA King Sudhodana, the Buddha's father. Page 74

SUSANOO Japanese goddess of the sea and storms, born from Izanagi's nose. Page 17

TSUKIYOMI Japanese goddess of the Moon, born from Izanagi's right eye. Page 17

VARUNA Hindu god of the sky, air and sea. Pages 52-3

VASUDEVA Husband of Devaki, and father of Krishna. Pages 54-6

VASUKI In Hindu mythology, one of several powerful kings of the snake gods (called nagas). Pages 13, 14, 15

VIRACOCHA The creator god of the Incas who ruled over much of South America in the 15th century AD. Page 25

VISHNU One of the three gods of the Hindu trinity (the three most important gods in Hinduism). Vishnu is the preserver. He is married to Lakshmi. Pages 11-15, 31, 54-6

YAMA Hindu god of death. Pages 52-3

YASHODA Wife of cowherd, Nanda, and Krishna's foster father. Page 56

ZIUSDRA In the ancient religion of Babylon, Ziusdra played the same part as Noah and Nuh. Pages 27-9